The
Northern Copper
Inuit

The
Civilization of the
American Indian
Series

THE
NORTHERN
COPPER
INUIT

A HISTORY

By Richard G. Condon
with Julia Ogina and the Holman Elders

Foreword by Nellie Cournoyea

University of Oklahoma Press : Norman and London

Published with the assistance of the National Endowment for the Humanities, a federal agency which supports the study of such fields as history, philosophy, literature, and language.

Library of Congress Cataloging-in-Publication Data

Condon, Richard G. (Richard Guy)
   The northern Copper Inuit : a history / by Richard G. Condon with Julia Ogina and the Holman elders ; foreword by Nellie Cournoyea.
       p.   cm.—(The civilization of the American Indian series ; v. 220)
   Includes bibliographical references and index.
   ISBN 0-8061-2811-9 (alk. paper)
   1. Copper Eskimos—History. 2. Copper Eskimos—Antiquities. 3. Copper Eskimos—Social conditions. 4. Social change—Northwest Territories—Victoria Island. 5. Victoria Island (N.W.T.)—History. 6. Victoria Island (N.W.T.)—Social conditions. I. Ogina, Julia. II. Title. III. Series.
   E99.E7C7284   1996
   971.9'2004971—dc20   95-39186
                                                                        CIP

The Northern Copper Inuit: A History is volume 220 in The Civilization of the American Indian Series.

1 2 3 4 5 6 7 8 9 10

Contents

Illustrations

Maps

All maps are by the author unless otherwise indicated.

Foreword

RESPECTED FRIEND and colleague Richard Condon has spent much of the past seventeen years visiting and conducting research in the northern Copper Inuit community of Holman. During this time, he has immersed himself in the culture, drunk tea and eaten bannock with the elders, and listened to old-time stories passed down through countless generations of Kangiryu-armiut. Sad to say, Richard Condon will not be continuing his work in Holman. He died September 7, 1995, while traveling in a walrus-skin boat near the town of Provideniya, Siberia. The accident that killed him and eight others was similar to those that have claimed arctic residents for generations.

The Northern Copper Inuit: A History was written after extensive research and consultation with the direct descendants of the earliest inhabitants of this far northern region. Mr. Condon's collaborative approach and effort not only will benefit the residents of Holman, but also will set a new standard for research and study in the Canadian North.

The responsibility of any respected historian is to record the political, social, and economic events of a particular society, nation, or culture for posterity. Mr. Condon's publication of *The Northern Copper Inuit: A History* skillfully achieves that objective wtih comprehensive authority.

Qujannamiik.

NELLIE COURNOYEA

Yellowknife
Northwest Territories, Canada

xiii

Preface

THE ULUKHAKTOKMIUT, the northernmost group of Copper Inuit, currently reside in the community of Holman. The ancestors of the Ulukhaktokmiut traditionally inhabited the area of Prince Albert Sound, Minto Inlet, and the south coast of Banks Island. Before the creation of the Holman settlement (in 1939) and the subsequent concentration of the population (in the 1960s), these people referred to themselves as the Kangiryuarmiut (people of Prince Albert Sound) and the Kangiryuarjatmiut (people of Minto Inlet). The term *Ulukhaktokmiut* is a recent designation, used by Holman residents when they describe themselves in Inuinnaqtun, the Copper Inuit dialect. Ulukhaktok is the large bluff which overlooks the community and surrounding areas. In Inuinnaqtun, *ulukhaktok* means "the place where *ulu* parts are found," referring to the sharp slate that traditionally was used to manufacture semilunar-shaped knives (or *ulus*).

The Ulukhaktokmiut are closely related to the Inuit of Coppermine and Cambridge Bay. All of these groups are referred to as Copper Inuit. The name—a Western designation—derives from the groups' traditional practice of manufacturing hunting tools and other implements out of native copper, which is found in great abundance in certain areas of Copper Inuit territory (see map 1 for location of Copper Inuit territory in the early nineteenth century). In terms of language and tradition, all of these groups represent a single—and unique—Inuit culture that

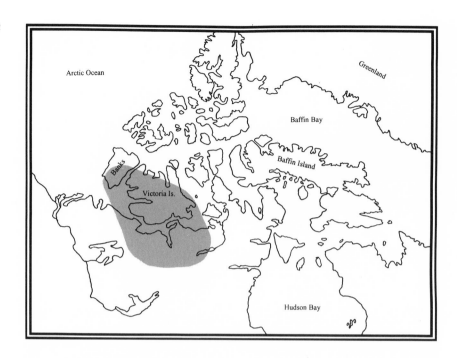

Map 1. Region occupied by Copper Inuit, early nineteenth century (source: Damas 1984:398).

extended from Stapylton Bay in the west to Perry River in the east. At the time of initial contact with Europeans, the total Copper Inuit population was estimated at between 800 and 1,000, spread over a vast area of arctic tundra. Approximately 200 to 250 of these people lived in the Holman region. Prior to European contact, the various groups of Copper Inuit had no common term by which to refer to themselves, although they did have a shared dialect and similar cultural traditions. They used local designations, each incorporating the suffix *-miut*, which means "people of." Those people who were classified in the same group, such as the Kangiryuarmiut of Prince Albert Sound or the Haneragmiut of southern Victoria Island, usually shared the same general summer range for hunting and fishing. Estimates of the number of precontact groupings vary between fourteen and nineteen. A reasonable estimate for the entire Copper Inuit region would be sixteen to seventeen.

The Inuit of this region are permanently enshrined in the anthropological literature as the Copper Eskimo; however, we decided that the modern designation, *Copper Inuit*, would be

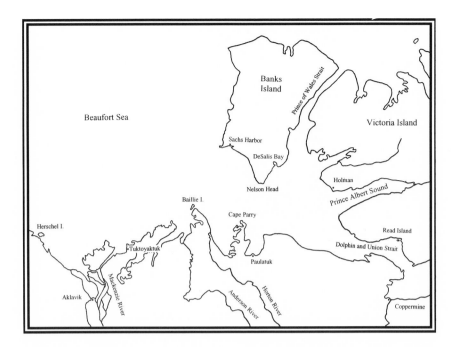

Map 2. The western Canadian Arctic, showing location of the Holman Region.

more appropriate in this text.[1] In this manner, we defer to the sensibilities of many Holman residents who find the term *Eskimo* offensive. This should not be interpreted as a blanket condemnation of the older, more widely recognized term. Within the fields of archaeology and cultural anthropology, there are excellent reasons for continued use of the term *Eskimo*. The most important of these is that Eskimo can be used when referring to the Inuit of northern Canada as well as the Yupik of southwestern Alaska. It is also worth noting that many Holman residents, especially elders, continue to use *Eskimo* when speaking English, and use *Inuit* when speaking Inuinnaqtun. Nevertheless, we believe that the people of Holman should be designated using a term from their own language rather than one derived from a subarctic Algonquian dialect (specifically Mon-

1. Vilhjalmur Stefansson (1919:33) is often credited with naming the Copper Eskimo, due to the extensive use of cold-hammered copper in many of their implements. Although Stefansson no doubt popularized the term, an earlier use can be found in Schwatka (1884:534).

tagnais) and purported to mean "eaters of raw meat." We also feel that whatever value this work may have as an educational text for young Inuit in Holman and other northern communities may be partly undermined through use of a term whose meaning can easily be misinterpreted.

This book represents the result of a cooperative effort between the authors and the residents of Holman to produce a complete documentation of the history and development of the Holman region from prehistoric times to the present. Over a period of seven years, beginning in 1987, extensive archival research, oral history interviews, and identification of historical photographs were conducted in order to reconstruct as accurately as possible the social, economic, and political changes that occurred in this region of the Arctic. We also spent a great deal of time (primarily in the summer of 1989) collecting genealogical information from elders. Although this document is primarily a community history, the processes of social change that are described in the book are to some degree applicable to other areas of the Canadian Arctic.

The authors would like to thank the following organizations and institutions for assisting at various stages of this research project: the Canadian Embassy to the United States, the Prince of Wales Northern Heritage Centre, the Northwest Territories (NWT) Department of Culture and Communications, the Science Institute of the NWT, the University of Arkansas Faculty Development Program, the National Endowment for the Humanities Travel to Collections Program, the American Council of Learned Societies, the Holman Hamlet Council, the Holman Eskimo Cooperative, and the Holman Elders Committee. We wish to thank all the elders of Holman for their time and cooperation. We are especially grateful to Nicholas Uluariuk, Sam Oliktoak, Rene Taipana, Flossie Papidluk, Ruth Nigiyonak, Frank Kuptana, Albert Palvik, Morris Nigiyok, Esau Elgayak, Agnes Nanogak Goose, Alec Banksland, Agnes Nigiyok, and Jimmy Memogana.

It is our regret that this oral history research project was not initiated nine years earlier, when Richard G. Condon, the senior of the book's two principal authors, first arrived in Holman. Since that time (1978), a great many elders have died, taking with them knowledge and memories of the past that should have been recorded for future generations. It is hoped that this modest work will revive the memory of these individuals and stimulate in their grandchildren and great-grandchildren a renewed interest, pride, and respect for their cultural heritage.

One of the more difficult aspects in conducting this research has been determining the most appropriate orthography to use for writing the Inuit language. For the Holman dialect of Inuinnaqtun, there are presently two orthographies in use: the Anglican orthography and the ILC (Inuvialuit Language Commission) orthography.[2] The Anglican orthography is the older of the two and was initially developed by early missionaries for use in hymnals and prayer books. The more recent ILC orthography was developed between 1981 and 1983. It conforms as closely as possible to the Inuit Cultural Institute's standard orthography for all Canadian Inuit dialects. While the ILC orthography is a more accurate representation of sounds made in Inuinnaqtun (and the one favored by the authors), most Holman residents who continue to speak and/or write Inuinnaqtun with any regularity prefer the older Anglican system.[3] The most significant difference between these two writing systems is the introduction of the *q* and double vowels in the ILC orthography. The ILC system also drops the unnecessary letters *o* and *e*. It is understandable that people would be resistant to changing a way of spelling that they have used since childhood, and we

2. Over the last twenty years, there has been an increase in the number of designations for dialects of the Inuit (or Eskimo) language. To the uninitiated, these terms can be most confusing, leading some to believe that differences in dialect are profound differences in language. It is generally recognized that the language of the Inuit is made up of a number of interrelated dialects. In the eastern Canadian Arctic, the term *Inuktitut* (sometimes *Inuttitut*) is most often used to refer to the Inuit language. In the Kitikmeot region of the central Canadian Arctic, the term *Inuinnaqtun* is preferred, and it is not uncommon to hear people refer to themselves as Inuinnaq (or, more appropriately, Inuinnait) as well as Inuit. In the western Canadian Arctic, the term *Inuvialuktun* is used to refer to the western Arctic dialect, while *Inuvialuit* is used to refer to the region's Inuit residents. Holman is in a curious position because some of its residents (those whose families originated in the western Arctic) continue to refer to themselves as Inuvialuit and their language as Inuvialuktun, even though the majority of Holman residents speak the central Arctic dialect, Inuinnaqtun. The most important thing for readers to remember is that all these dialects, from North Alaska to Greenland, are considered by linguists to be one language.

3. An updated version of the Anglican orthography was issued in 1972 with the publication of Bishop John Sperry's translations of the Gospels and Acts of the Apostles. This version is closer to the ICI orthography although it does not use the *q* and *r* found in the latter. Nevertheless, many Holman residents continue to prefer the pre-1972 orthography (Rev. Tim Chesterton, personal communication).

have occasionally been criticized for using the ILC orthography. Many people view it as a foreign intrusion upon their writing system. To deal with this problem, we have decided to write all proper names of individuals and widely recognized geographical locations (such as Ulukhaktok) using the older Anglican orthography (as preferred by many residents). In those cases where we feel it appropriate, we have included an alternate ICI spelling in parentheses. For most other Inuinnaqtun words, we have opted for the ILC orthography, using as our guide the Kangiryuarmiut dictionary (*Kangiryuarmiut Uqauhingita Numiktittitdjutingit*) published in 1983 by Ronald Lowe, of Laval University. This, we feel, constitutes a suitable compromise.

Spelling of the place-name Ulukhaktok is a case in point. If one wanders about the community of Holman, it is easy to encounter six or seven alternate spellings of this word on signs and buildings. Families originally from the western Arctic will state that the proper spelling is Uluksartok; local families will offer one of the versions without an *s*, such as Ulukhaktok or Oluhaktok. In earlier drafts of the manuscript for this book the authors used Ulukhaqtuuk as the Inuinnaqtun designation for the community. In response to some criticism, Condon approached the hamlet council in July 1991 and requested that a resolution be passed regarding the official Inuinnaqtun spelling of three designations: Ulukhaktok, Ulukhaktokmiut, and Kangiryuarmiut. After some discussion, the council passed a formal resolution requesting that all future correspondence, letterheads, and community signs conform to the officially adopted spellings.

Another orthographic difficulty has been the spelling of proper names of individuals long deceased. Although we have been able to check some spellings with living descendants, this has not been possible in all cases. Living descendants may, for example, reside elsewhere or may simply not know the proper spelling of an ancestor's name. While certain figures are mentioned in the published literature or in Hudson's Bay Company (HBC) journals, there is very rarely any consistency in spelling. We have tried our best to seek out the proper spellings of such names, often providing alternate spellings in parentheses. Although we have tried our best to be conscientious in this regard, there will no doubt be a few proper names that are not spelled to the satisfaction of all. To the dissatisfied, we offer our deepest apologies.

Over the seven years of our research and interviewing, we accumulated a wealth of material from Holman elders. Most of our interviews were extremely wide ranging, including photograph identification, recall of genealogical information, and recording of life-history material. Because of the tendency of some elders to jump rapidly from one topic to another, we have had to exercise a heavy hand in the editing of interview transcripts. Originally we planned to include unedited interview transcripts but this has not been possible. A typical interview might start out with some photograph identification, continue with a discussion of a historical event, jump to the collection of genealogical material, and return to photograph identification. A life-history story abandoned abruptly during one interview session might not be continued until the next session. Many elders tended to jump around in time when telling stories, a tendency that made it very difficult to reconstruct historical events in a linear fashion. We extracted from the interviews the narratives we feel to be the most interesting and informative. In some situations, little editing was required; in others, we had to piece together information from several sessions. In doing so, we tried to preserve the spirit of what each elder had communicated about his or her life and experiences. The interview excerpts appear at intervals in the book to complement photographs and main text.

All interviews were tape-recorded in Holman, generally in the elders' homes. Both of us participated in these interview sessions. Julia Ogina provided both translation and later transcription of the interviews. The editing of the interviews and their incorporation into the text was done by Rick Condon.

When the manuscript was almost complete we decided to include excerpts of interviews with William Kuptana of Sachs Harbour. These interviews were done in 1988 and 1989 by Allice Legat of the NWT Department of Culture and Communications as part of a separate project. The transcripts are presently held by the NWT Archives at the Prince of Wales Northern Heritage Centre. Kuptana was originally from the Holman region and we decided that it would be appropriate to include his recollections along with those of the Holman elders we had ourselves interviewed. We would like to thank Sarah Kuptana of Sachs Harbour and her family for allowing us to reproduce some of this interview material.

Preface   We regret not being able to interview all the elders of Holman nor being able to include in this work all the narratives provided by those elders who *were* interviewed. In conducting our interviews, we selected what we felt was a representative sample of elders. Others undoubtedly have much worthwhile knowledge of the region's history. Although time and money prevented us from recording them, it is our hope that future oral history projects will preserve what they have to say as well.

RICHARD G. CONDON
JULIA OGINA

The
Northern Copper
Inuit

1. Prehistory of the Holman Region

The Origin of the Ulukhaktokmiut

LONG BEFORE the ancestors of modern Inuit set foot on Victoria Island, the Canadian Arctic had been inhabited by a number of different peoples and cultures. The first people to live year-round in the Canadian Arctic are referred to as the Paleoeskimos (literally "old Eskimos"). Since these people left behind small and finely chipped stone tools, archaeologists have named their culture the Arctic Small Tool Tradition (ASTt).

Archaeological evidence indicates that the Arctic Small Tool tradition first appeared in Alaska around four to five thousand years ago and spread quickly throughout the Canadian Arctic and Greenland (Maxwell 1984:359; 1985:43). The origin of the ASTt Paleoeskimos is still open to some debate, although similarities between ASTt artifacts and those found in Siberia suggest that the ASTt Paleoeskimos came from Northeastern Siberia and crossed to Alaska either by boat or on foot, across the shifting winter ice of the Bering Strait (McGhee 1983:75). Once established in Alaska, the Paleoeskimos moved northward into North Alaska and then eastward into the Canadian Arctic. The Paleoeskimo expansion into Arctic Canada occurred during a warming trend, and part of the migration may have been by boat (Maxwell 1960). Since these regions of northern Canada were not inhabited by any other peoples, the Paleoeskimos found a virgin territory full of game and ripe for exploitation. One speculation is that the Paleoeskimos migrated eastward

Fig. 1.1. *The Little Hunter*, Holman Print Collection, 1982. Stonecut by Helen Kalvak (artist) and Harry Egotak (printer). Edition: 40. Courtesy of the Holman Eskimo Cooperative.

by relying upon the hunting of musk oxen, a resource that was quickly depleted due to the relative ease with which the animals could be slaughtered. Once established in the Canadian Arctic, however, the Paleoeskimos concentrated upon the hunting of caribou and seasonal hunting of seals (Dumond 1987:92). Interestingly, there is no evidence yet of the specialized hunting equipment associated with breathing-hole sealing on the winter ice.

Archaeological evidence suggests that the material culture of the ASTt Paleoeskimos was not a very elaborate or complex one, but was sufficient to allow the people to make a living by hunting seals, caribou, musk ox, and small game. One important item that the Paleoeskimos brought with them was the bow and arrow, which was previously unknown in the New

Fig. 1.2. Small implements of the Paleoeskimos, 2000–1000 B.C. The Paleoeskimos of the Arctic Small Tool tradition were expert craftsmen who made detailed arrowheads, spear points, knife blades, and scrapers. From left to right: harpoon end-blade from Port Refuge, Devon Island, chert; nontoggling harpoon head from Port Refuge, Devon Island, ivory; toggling harpoon head from Pond Inlet, Baffin Island, antler; arrow point from Port Refuge, Devon Island, chert; side scraper from Port Refuge, Devon Island, chert; biface point from Port Refuge, Devon Island, chert. Courtesy of the Carnegie Museum of Natural History, Carnegie Institute, and the Canadian Museum of Civilization.

World. This important item of hunting technology obviously gave the Paleoeskimos a significant advantage in hunting large game on the open tundra (McGhee 1983:75). For marine-mammal hunting, the Paleoeskimos made use of both toggling and nontoggling harpoons. The toggling harpoon head was a particularly efficient invention, equipped with a basal spur that would force the harpoon head to turn sideways once embedded in the flesh of the animal. This weapon minimized the possibility of prey breaking loose after impact.

The ASTt Paleoeskimos did not build large houses: their dwellings probably held only a single family. Remains of these dwellings are often hard to spot on the tundra. They may consist only of a small pile of rocks that served as a cooking hearth. Archaeological evidence from Paleoeskimo living sites suggests that these people probably lived year-round in skin tents, oval to rectangular in shape, with a square hearth of stone slabs in

5

the center. For heat, a variety of fuel sources were used, among them driftwood, willow, and sea-mammal blubber. The ASTt Paleoeskimos used soapstone lamps, but such devices appear to have been fairly rare. A more common practice was the technique of burning chunks of fat and fatty bones on flat stones or wood and open hearths (Maxwell (1984:362). Archaeologists have not found snowknives or other implements that could be used for cutting snowblocks: therefore, it does not appear that the ASTt people used snowhouses.

The ASTt people were widespread throughout the Canadian Arctic, but only a small number of ASTt sites have been found on Victoria Island and Banks Island. McGhee (1978:49) speculates that the Umingmak site, on northern Banks Island, where the bone remains of hundreds of musk oxen are scattered over a large area in association with Paleoeskimo artifacts, represents the kills of a small band of hunters over several generations. Other Paleoeskimo sites, found near Wellington Bay on the southern coast of Victoria Island, provide evidence of cooperative caribou hunting. Stone markers appear to have been used to funnel caribou toward a kill site. The use of stone fences to drive caribou in cooperative hunting is virtually identical to the autumn caribou hunting practices of later Inuit groups. In fact, the stone fences built by the ASTt people were most likely repaired and reused by countless generations of both Paleoeskimos and Inuit up to the period of European contact. Thereafter, the introduction of firearms made such cooperative hunting unnecessary.

Approximately 3,500 years ago, the climate of the Canadian Arctic became noticeably cooler, a trend that continued until about A.D. 1. The alteration resulted in longer, colder winters and more severe ice conditions in arctic waters. The tree line retreated south. These changing conditions probably contributed to the reduction in the number of land and sea mammals. The regions of the High Arctic became depopulated and may even have been abandoned entirely as the ASTt Paleoeskimos—dependent on animal life for their survival—moved southward to the Low Arctic. This new zone of Paleoeskimo exploitation extended as far south as Great Slave Lake, Lake Athabaska, and northern Manitoba (McGhee 1983:78).

The Dorset People

Between 3,000 and 2,500 years ago, major changes occurred in ASTt culture as the Paleoeskimos adapted to a colder climate, a culture now known as Dorset emerged. The Dorset culture was first identified in 1925 by the arctic anthropologist Diamond Jenness, who had been a member of the 1913–1918 Canadian Arctic Expedition (see chapter 2). While working at the National Museum of Canada in Ottawa, Jenness was sent a collection of artifacts that had recently been discovered near Cape Dorset on Baffin Island, and immediately realized that the artifacts were unlike anything that had been discovered before. Jenness named this culture the Dorset tradition, after the Cape Dorset community.

There is little doubt that the Dorset people were direct descendants of the ASTt Paleoeskimos and that the Dorsets had developed a culture better suited to colder climatic conditions. There is general agreement that the transition from ASTt to Dorset occurred between 800 B.C. and 500 B.C. (Maxwell 1984:363). The oral traditions of modern Inuit are full of stories about the Tunnit—the people of the distant past. Such stories are undoubtedly the result of direct contact with ancient peoples like the Dorset—stories that have been handed down through the generations. Maxwell (1985) records the Inuit fascination with the people who lived in the Canadian Arctic before their arrival:

> They are said to be dwarfs, or giants, with prodigious strength. . . . According to the stories, the Tunnit, since they had no sled dogs, used this prodigious strength to drag killed walrus home using only a small single-man sled (The archaeological evidence is that among the Dorset, dogs were very scarce and only small hand-drawn sleds were used). They loved their wives dearly and dragging such a 500-kg weight at the end of the day seemed like child's play, so anxious were they to return to their wives. When they went breathing hole hunting they took their small soapstone lamps [many Dorset lamps are very small], set them burning under their parkas, and then pinned the skirts of the parkas to the snow. When seal appeared, they jumped up in excitement and consequently spilled burning oil over their stomachs. As a result, most of the men's stomachs were scalded and scarred. At night they did not sleep on broad sleeping platforms as the Inuit do, but crawled into little semi-subterranean houses where they slept on narrow benches with their legs extended up the side higher than their heads (Maxwell 1985:128).

The core area of this evolution from the ASTt was in the region around the Foxe Basin, northern Hudson Bay, and Hudson Strait. Since the change in climate resulted in more extensive ice conditions during most of the winter, the Dorset Paleoeskimos were heavily dependent upon the hunting of seals through the mammal's breathing holes. Compared with the ASTt people, the Dorsets were sedentary. They focused more on coastal areas, hunting for marine mammals, rather than hunting inland for caribou and musk oxen. This is perhaps why so few Dorset sites have been found in inland areas (Dumond 1987:97). The lowered dependence upon land mammals was most likely the result of colder and more unstable climatic conditions with an increase in precipitation. Dekin (1975) believes that the climatic conditions led to a decline in the numbers of caribou and musk oxen, which depended on foraging for winter survival.

The presence of snowknives in Dorset sites suggests that these people regularly made and used snowhouses, especially at those times of year when people were out on the ice engaged in breathing-hole sealing. Snowhouses were undoubtedly lighted and heated by soapstone lamps, which were commonly used by the

Fig. 1.3. Artist's depiction of a Dorset winter dwelling (1000 B.C. to A.D. 1000). Evidence from archaeological sites suggests that the Dorset people lived in semisubterranean houses with sod walls and skin roofs. These dwellings may have been shared by several families. The Dorset people may have also built and used snowhouses for the midwinter months. Illustration by James Senior. Source: Jacobs and Richardson 1983:80. Courtesy of the Carnegie Museum of Natural History, Carnegie Institute.

Dorset people. Dorset peoples also constructed large, semisubterranean, sod-banked houses that were covered with skins.
These semisubterranean structures probably housed several
families, were probably occupied during the fall and early winter before people moved out onto the ice to live in snowhouses.
Another significant development of the Dorset Paleoeskimos
was the use of small sleds with ivory runners. They also built
kayaks for open-water hunting.

Oddly, use of the bow and arrow seems to have declined and
eventually disappeared during the Dorset period. Hunting of
the dwindling herds of caribou and musk oxen appears to have
been accomplished with lances and spears. Whereas the earlier,
ASTt people stalked caribou in midwinter, using both dogs
and bow and arrow, the Dorset people rarely engaged in such
activity. Most of the Dorset's caribou hunting seems to have
been conducted in the warmer months, when animals could be
driven into lakes and speared by hunters in kayaks (Maxwell
1984:365). A high concentration of caribou bones has been found
near lakeshore sites, suggesting that this was common practice
during the Dorset period.

Another important item of ASTt technology that dropped out
of use during the Dorset period was the drill, an instrument
used to make holes in hunting tools and other implements.
Throughout a thousand-year span of Dorset technology, there
is no evidence of drilled holes. All holes in hard materials were
laboriously scratched out (Maxwell 1985:128). The decline and
disappearance of the bow and arrow can be explained (as noted
above) but the disappearance of the drill remains a mystery.
Given these changes—loss of the drill, bow and arrow, and
dogs—it might appear that the Dorset people were less well
adapted than their predecessors to arctic living (Meldgaard
1962). Nevertheless, archaeological evidence indicates that the
Dorsets survived for well over fifteen hundred years.

Although there was a certain amount of regional variation in
Dorset subsistence practices, the general pattern in their core
area was very similar to that of later Inuit residents. Spring and
summer was spent along the coast, hunting walrus and seal, either from kayaks or on the landfast ice. Families appear to have
been spread out along the coast rather than concentrated in large
communities. Later in the summer, however, families would
gather at favored fishing locations and at places where caribou
herds could be driven into lakes. At this time of year, the primary
shelter would have been the skin tent. In the autumn, families
returned to the coast and their semisubterranean houses, and

continued the hunting of marine mammals. Once the ice was solid, most Dorset groups moved out on the sea.

Remains of Dorset Paleoeskimos can be found throughout the Holman region. Numerous tent rings and food caches made of stone are evidence that the Dorset people wandered western Victoria Island long before ancestors of the Inuit entered the region. Remains of one of the largest known Dorset longhouses can be found on the north shore of Prince Albert Sound, near the mouth of the Kuuk River. There are only a handful of these longhouses in the Canadian Arctic and they are an object of great speculation. Evidence suggests that they were built sometime between A.D. 500 and A.D. 1,000, toward the end of the Dorset period. The longhouse on Victoria Island is 32 meters long and 7 meters wide, its sides constructed of large boulders and stone slabs. Evidence suggests that it was built around A.D. 500. As is the case with other Dorset longhouses, there is no indication that it ever had a roof, and there is very little cultural material within it, suggesting that it was not used as a residence. The Victoria Island longhouse may have been used for ceremonial purposes and/or community feasts (McGhee 1978:67).

The Inuagulgit

Frank Kuptana. Those large houses were built by people known as Inuagulgit—small people, with big houses. People from around here refer to them as Inuagulgit. Those people are still around, at places like Quaraukat [Kaoraokat]. Their houses are still being built. People can hear them making noises sometimes. They were also known by the Kangiryuarmiut as Pulayuqat—small people. Their bows and arrows were too big for them. They would drag them on the ground when they went hunting caribou. That's how the elders told us stories about them. The Kangiryuarmiut referred to them as Pulayuqat and Inuagulgit. Once, some people were walking and came across them and startled them. Everyone left into the ground, those Pulayuqat. They left behind a baby, and those people who were walking picked up the baby. They started to kiss the baby and said that the baby had a strong scent of baby smell, which left those people who kissed it smelling like a baby. They put the baby back down on the ground and discussed the baby and the Pulayuqat. The next thing they knew, the baby was gone. Those people who had gone had picked their baby up. They say the baby was a very cute baby too. Those Kangiryuarmiut people sure scared those Pulayuqat.

10

Fig. 1.4. Dorset longhouse. This is one of the largest Dorset longhouses in the Canadian Arctic. It is located on the north shore of Prince Albert Sound, near the mouth of the Kuuk River. It measures 32 meters long and 7 meters wide. The walls were built with large boulders and slabs of stone. There is no indication that it ever had a roof and it may have been used as a temporary ceremonial structure. Artifacts found within the structure indicate that it was probably built around A.D. 500. Although archaeologists are in agreement that structures such as this were built by the Dorset people, many Holman elders have a different explanation for their origin. According to Inuit legend, they were built by people called the Inuagulgit (also known as Pulayaqat)— a small people who had the ability to disappear into the ground when frightened. Some elders believe that the Inaugulgit still exist and continue to build stone structures that can be seen in the Holman area. Courtesy of the Canadian Museum of Civilization, No. J-19342-2.

Those [Pulayuqat] people never came back after they left, but those houses are still being built, but just a little bit smaller.

Other archaeological remains of the Dorset culture show that the Dorset Paleoeskimos were expert carvers and artists. Most of their art seems to have been concerned with the supernatural. There is evidence of a shamanism, burial practices, and magic (Taylor and Swinton 1967:44). The Dorsets made fine, highly

Fig. 1.5. Dorset mask from Button Point, Bylot Island, NWT. The Dorset people were expert artisans and carvers of wood, bone, and antler and their highly developed art indicates a preoccupation with the spiritual world. Masks such as this may have been used by Dorset shamans—an attempt to control the supernatural. Photo by Stan Franzos. Source: Jacobs and Richardson 1983. Courtesy of the Carnegie Museum of Natural History, Carnegie Institute.

detailed carvings of wood, bone, antler, ivory, and soapstone. Surviving carvings include masks (both large and miniature) and small amulets of animals, such as seals and polar bears. At some Dorset sites, ornamented caribou antlers have been found, covered with clusters of as many as sixty human faces (Maxwell 1985:163). The Dorsets made carvings representing just about every kind of mammal, bird, and fish in their environment, including the sculpin. But more than half of the discovered carvings are of polar bears and humans. These animal figures may have been ascribed magical powers to assist in hunting and fishing.

During the height of the Dorset period, the Dorset culture spread from northern Hudson Bay to the western Canadian Arctic, the Keewatin, the High Arctic, and Greenland, and as far south as southern Labrador. In southern Labrador, the Dorsets crossed to Newfoundland, where they were the principal occupants between 2,500 and 1,500 years ago. The Dorsets thus showed an ability to adapt to a forested environment as well as an arctic environment (McGhee 1983:82). Between A.D. 500 and A.D. 1000, however, the Dorsets in Newfoundland were replaced by ancestors of the Beothuk Indians. It is not known whether the Dorsets were killed by the Beothuks or became extinct just before the Beothuks arrived.

By A.D. 1000, the Dorsets had developed a culture superbly adapted to the harsh Canadian Arctic. Soon, however, the Dorset Paleoeskimos and their culture disappeared. Two major developments may account for this dramatic disappearance. The first was a warming trend. This commenced sometime after A.D. 500 and from A.D. 900 to A.D. 1200 the temperatures throughout the Arctic were much warmer than those of today. This warming trend resulted in significant changes in precipitation and sea-ice conditions. Since the Dorsets had developed a culture heavily dependent upon on sea-mammal hunting on ice, it is possible that they were unable to adjust, as the climate change altered the distribution of animals. Many Dorset groups may have starved to death; others may have died out due to lowered birth rates.

The second major development was the appearance of a new group of people from the west—the Thule people (sometimes called Neoeskimos). The Thule are recognized by archaeologists as the true ancestors of modern Inuit. According to archaeologist Robert McGhee (1983:84):

Inuit legends state that when their ancestors arrived in Arctic Canada, they found the area occupied by another race, the Tuniit,

13

whom with fair confidence we can identify with the Dorset people known through archaeology. Although the legends often tell of good relations between the Inuit and the Tuniit, usually described as a large and gentle race of people who lacked bows and other items of technology, they inevitably end with the Tuniit being killed or driven from their native land.

The Thule Expansion into Arctic Canada

While the Dorset people of Canada and Greenland were quietly and efficiently exploiting the resources of the Arctic, a series of whale hunting cultures developed in the coastal regions of Alaska. These cultures were oriented toward the hunting of large sea mammals such as whales and walrus from oceangoing umiaks. The most significant technological development of these cultures was the float harpoon—an inflatable sealskin float attached to a harpoon head. Using the float, it was no longer necessary to hold onto a wounded animal with a line, made of animal skin and attached to the harpoon. Rather, a sea mammal could be harpooned with one or more floats and followed until it became exhausted. It was the development of this technology that made possible the intensive hunting of large marine mammals.

By A.D. 1000, one of these cultures, the Thule, was firmly established on the north coast of Alaska (The name Thule—pronounced "too-lay"—is derived from a community in northwest Greenland, where Thule remains have been found). The Thule Neoeskimos represented the ultimate whale-hunting culture. While earlier Alaskan cultures had occasionally taken the large bowhead whale, the Thule people, equipped with the float harpoon, became extremely proficient at hunting this large animal. Around A.D. 1000, with the climate of the North American Arctic growing ever warmer, the Thule people began moving westward from North Alaska into Arctic Canada. As the extensive cover of winter ice that made up the Dorset people's seal-hunting platforms receded, open water became more widespread in the central and eastern regions of the Canadian Arctic. Bowhead whales, which migrated each spring along the north coast of Alaska, started to head deeper into the waters of northern Canada. As the great bowheads headed eastward, they were followed by the Thule people, who spread themselves, like the ASTt Paleoeskimos before them, throughout the Canadian Arctic, all the way into West and East Greenland and down the coast of Labrador (Dumond (1987:141).

The spread of the Thule people is one of the more remarkable migrations in human history. In less than two hundred years, the Thule people and their culture reached from Alaska into the Canadian Arctic and Greenland. By A.D. 1400, most of the Canadian Arctic above the tree line was inhabited by these newcomers (McGhee 1983:88). In some areas, the Thule people may have come into contact with Dorset groups. Archaeologists know very little about the exact nature of this contact, although there is much speculation. Some Dorset people may have been absorbed by the dominant Thule; others may have simply died out. There is no evidence that the Thule slaughtered the Dorset people, who were on their way to extinction anyway because of their inability to adapt to the warmer conditions. The Thule, better adapted to marine-mammal hunting in open water, adopted a number of items of Dorset technology, including snowknives, snowhouses, soapstone lamps, and cooking pots. The Thule for their own part reintroduced the bow and arrow to the Canadian Arctic.

Prehistory of the Holman Region

One reason for the Thule's success was their great mobility. In addition to using large umiaks for summer travel on the ocean, the Thule had dogs and long sleds for winter travel. While the Dorsets did not travel much more than a day's journey from their camps in search of food, the Thule ranged over wide areas in search of animals (Maxwell 1985:240). This thirst for travel foreshadowed that of modern-day Inuit.

The Thule people are best known for building semisubterranean houses with raised sleeping platforms and sunken entrances. In parts of the Canadian Arctic, the Thule built these houses with rock walls and flagstone floors. Whalebone rafters supported roofs of skins and turf. In many areas, Thule houses are easy to identify because of large amounts of whalebone spread about. There is also evidence that some of the Thule people made and used snowhouses as well.

Originally attracted to the Canadian Arctic by the movements of the bowhead whale, once entrenched the Thule began to exploit other food sources. As they expanded, the Thule people entered areas far from the migratory routes of the bowheads, and they had to rely more on walrus, narwhals, seals, belugas, fish, caribou, and musk oxen. Archaeological evidence supports such a theory. In the Holman region, for example, there is evidence of seal hunting from kayaks in open water or from the floe edge as the primary subsistence activity, probably supplemented by fishing and caribou hunting (McGhee 1972:54).

An important site from the Thule period in the Holman region is the Memorana site (named after Jimmy Memogana of Holman), located approximately nine miles to the southeast of Holman. This site, excavated in the 1960s, represents a winter settlement of four houses. These houses were constructed of stone and turf and probably had wooden poles supporting a sod roof (McGhee 1972:24). Unlike other houses from the Thule period, these dwellings were not dug into the ground (semisubterranean) but were built at ground level. Each house had an entrance passage measuring from eight to ten feet in length, but there is no evidence that these passageways were constructed at an incline to keep out the cold. Such inclined entrances were

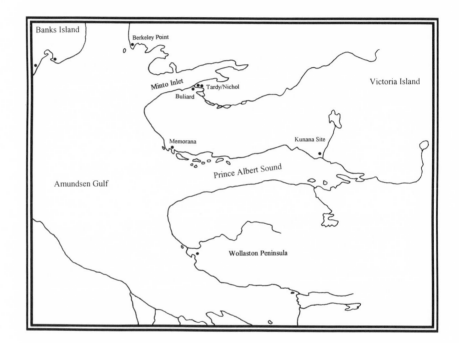

Map 3. Location of major archaeological sites on western Victoria Island. There are literally hundreds of archaeological sites on western Victoria Island and this map shows only a few of those mentioned in the text. The Memorana and Berkeley Point sites (Thule period) were occupied sometime between A.D. 1200 and 1500. The Nichol, Tardy, and Buliard sites (all located near the mouth of the Kuujjuak River) are from the intermediate period, between the Thule and early historic periods (or about A.D. 1600–1800). The Kunana site, on Prince Albert Sound, is much more recent, site dated to the early nineteenth century.

a common feature of Thule houses in other areas. While the
Thule houses in the Eastern Arctic and the High Arctic often
made use of whalebone for construction (for example, rib-bones
used as rafters), the Memorana dwellings were constructed
solely from stone, turf, and driftwood. Both floors and sleeping
platforms were made from limestone slabs. Artifacts from the
Memorana site include a wide array of seal-hunting equipment,
land-hunting equipment, fishing implements, soapstone vessel
fragments, dolls, carvings, and pottery fragments. The Memorana site—dated between A.D. 1200 and 1400 (McGhee 1972:39)—
appears to have been occupied primarily during the winter.
Since the climate was considerably warmer than it is today,
the hunters who lived at this site must have been able to hunt
seals in open water throughout much of the winter. There is
no evidence that the Thule people of the Holman region lived
in large snowhouse communities on the ocean ice, engaged in
breathing-hole sealing, as did the Copper Inuit of the historic
period.

As time went on, the Thule people developed regional differences in their social and economic activities, eventually giving
rise to the distinct Inuit groups encountered by early European
explorers. These groups came to be known as the Copper, Netsil-
ilk, Iglulik, and Aivilik. McGhee (1983:90) notes: "When 18th
and 19th century European explorers and anthropologists began to penetrate the region, they found no widespread and
uniform culture like that of the Thule people. Rather, they
encountered small and more or less isolated groups of Inuit
with a great variety of adaptations to local environments." The
most important event giving rise to these distinct Inuit groups
was another change in climate. The warming trend which had
initiated the Thule expansion lasted only a few centuries and
sometime after A.D. 1200 the climate began a gradual cooling.
Around 1600, this cooling became dramatic and by 1850 the
climate was much harsher than is today's (McGhee 1983:91).
In the face of the new conditions, the Thule people in most
areas underwent significant adaptation. These changes, however, were not uniform. In North Alaska and southern Labrador,
adaptation was less dramatic because people still had access
to open water which allowed continuation of whale hunting
(Dumond 1987:147). In the Central Arctic, including the Holman region, the impact of climatic cooling was much more
dramatic and resulted in a pronounced change in hunting activities. Midwinter hunting of seals and other marine mammals

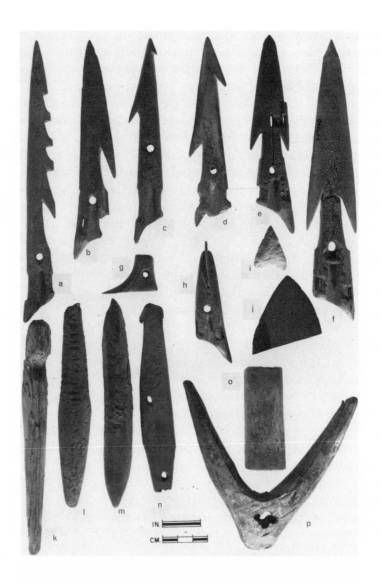

Fig. 1.6. A range of sea-hunting tools from the Memorana
site, Prince Albert Sound. All Thule-type harpoon heads
and related tools, they were probably used primarily for
the hunting of ring seals and bearded seals. In alphabeti-
cal order: (a–f) harpoon heads; (g) harpoon finger rest;
(h) harpoon head; (i) harpoon endblade; (k) throat plug
(unconfirmed identification); (l–m) harpoon icepick (unconfirmed identification); (n) darting harpoon head; (o)
harpoon foreshaft socket; (p) umiak harpoon rest.
Source: McGhee 1972:26. Courtesy of the Canadian Museum of Civilization, No. J-19968-6.

in open water was abandoned entirely, as people were forced to spend their winters on the ocean ice in snowhouse communities engaged in breathing-hole sealing. Summers were spent in small family groups, hunting and fishing in the interior. This was the typical and varied pattern of hunting and fishing activity that characterized the Copper Inuit at the time European explorers began to enter the region.

Important post-Thule sites can be found close to Holman. Three of these are located at the mouth of the Kuujjuak River: the Buliard, Nichol, and Tardy sites. These remains have been dated between the Thule period and the historic period, or approximately A.D. 1600 to 1800. This is often referred to as the Intermediate Interval. The three sites are all close to one another and contain a total of fourteen lightly constructed semisubterranean houses and forty-four heavy, oval tent rings. There is a paucity of other archeological remains. The semisubterranean structures all differ from Thule-period houses: there is no evidence of a raised sleeping platform, a stone floor, or use of heavy turf or sod for roofing. This suggests that the roof may have been made up of skins placed over a network of poles (McGhee 1972:58). A characteristic feature of the three sites is that they appear not to have been occupied in winter. They were probably used in the fall and then vacated when the community built winter snowhouses on the ice of Minto Inlet. This contrasts with the earlier Thule pattern of wintering along the coast in somewhat permanent, more solidly constructed houses like those found at the Memorana site. The pattern revealed in these Intermediate Interval sites is very similar to that documented by the earliest explorers into Copper Inuit territory in which breathing-hole sealing from snowhouse communities was already established. The climate change appears to have been the cause of the shift in strategy.

More recently—in the 1960s—another site in the Holman region was excavated: the Kunana site on the north shore of Prince Albert Sound. This dates from A.D. 1800 to 1900, a time when European explorers were entering the region and starting to trade with the Copper Inuit (see chapter 2).

The Kunana site—located on the west bank of the Kuuk River, approximately 200 yards from the mouth consists of the remains of seventy-two structures, most of them dwellings and caches. In the river directly in front of the site is a large fish weir, constructed of rocks. To the north and west, a complex series of caribou drive lanes appears to have been used to collect eastward-migrating caribou and funnel them into a kill site on

19

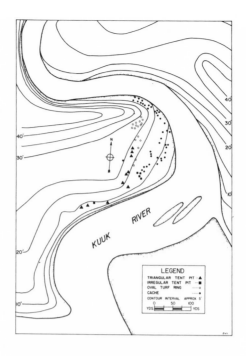

Map 4. The Kunana site, shown here in a bend of the Kuuk Riber on the north shore of Prince Albert Sound, is a recent post-Thule site. It was probably occupied by Ulukhaktom-iut ancestors between A.D. 1800 and 1900. Archaeological evidence suggests that this was a site of caribou hunting, used primarily during the fall. There is evidence of European materials at the site, indicating the beginning of European contact and trade (source: McGhee 1972:70–72).

the west side of the river (McGhee 1972:71; Taylor 1967: fig. 12). Since most of the bones excavated at the site (96 percent) are from caribou, it would appear that this was primarily an autumn caribou hunting location. Fishing was probably a secondary activity.

Of the seventy-two structures, forty-one are caches, constructed of large boulders. There are also tent pits and oval turf rings, both of which suggest that skin tents were the primary form of dwelling. Most of the artifacts from the Kunana site

Fig. 1.7. Aerial view of the stone alignments near
the Kunana site, Kuuk River, Victoria Island. Courtesy of the Canadian Museum of Civilization, No.
51265.

are very similar to ethnographic collections made by anthropologists and explorers in the opening decades of the twentieth
century. The presence of European materials such as wire, glass,
and tin suggests some trade with British exploration vessels
that entered the western Victoria Island region in the 1850s. It
is to this early contact that we now turn.

2. Early Contact History in the Holman Region

BECAUSE OF THEIR extreme isolation, the Copper Inuit of the Holman region were among the very last Canadian Inuit groups to be contacted by the outside world. The earliest known contact was extremely brief and occurred in the 1850s when two British naval expeditions entered Amundsen Gulf in search of the Northwest Passage. At that time, little was known in Europe or southern Canada about the Arctic islands. Most of the region had not yet been explored or mapped. Even the outline of Victoria Island was shrouded in mystery.

The first of the two British expeditions was by the *Investigator*, a ship under the command of Captain Robert McClure. The *Investigator* had sailed from the North Alaskan Coast, seeking a passage to the North Atlantic and hoping to discover evidence concerning the fate of the Sir John Franklin Expedition, which had been lost in the Arctic since 1840. On August 7, 1850, Mc-Clure reached the towering cliffs on the southern tip of Banks Island. Planting a flag, McClure claimed the island for Queen Victoria and named the imposing escarpment Lord Nelson Head (Berton 1988:219). Sailing up Prince of Wales Strait, a narrow passage separating Banks Island from Victoria Island, the *Investigator* was besieged by ice near the Princess Royal Islands, forcing McClure and his men to spend the winter of 1850/1851 locked in the ice. McClure sent out numerous sledg-

Fig. 2.1. *Gambling Game*, Holman Print Collection, 1984. Lithograph by Mark Emerak (artist) and Eddie Okheena (printer). Edition: 50. Courtesy of the Holman Eskimo Cooperative.

ing expeditions to the north and south in order to map the coastlines of Victoria and Banks Islands. In typically British naval fashion, all of these expeditions were done by foot, with crew members pulling their sledges without the assistance of dogs. One party, under the command of Robert Wynniatt, reached the large bay, now named after him, at the north end of Victoria Island; another, under the command of William Haswell, explored Walker Bay, Minto Inlet, and the north shore of Prince Albert Sound. Hanswell traveled to 114 degrees west longitude, which would have placed him ninety to one hundred miles east of the modern community of Holman. Haswell and his men explored most of the islands and coastline on the northwest side of Prince Albert Sound, including Holman Island and Investigator Island. It is quite possible that Haswell was responsible for assigning the name Holman to Holman Island.[1]

1. According to records at the Department of Energy, Mines, and Resources, Canada, Holman Island was named after John R. Holman, assistant surgeon on Edward Inglefield's two supply voyages (1853 and 1854) to Beechey Island

On one of the islands in the sound (probably Investigator Island), Haswell built a cairn and left a cylinder with a message in it.

On their return trip to the *Investigator*, Haswell's party encountered a group of Inuit at a location later named Berkeley Point. McClure noted in his journal:

> The whole coast was strewn with driftwood, and many vestiges of Esquimaux encampments were met with, but of a very old date. On returning, he [Haswell] was most surprised to find a party, consisting of eighteen natives, encamped on the ice a few miles from the northwest point of the northernmost inlet [Minto Inlet] in quest of seals; but not understanding each other, no information could be obtained. (McClure n.d.:70)

The meeting was friendly, culminating in an exchange of gifts. When Haswell returned to the *Investigator* several days later, he reported his discovery to McClure who, eager to talk with the Inuit, departed with an interpreter the following day to track them down. Accompanying McClure was Johann August Miertsching, a Moravian missionary from Labrador, fluent in the Inuit language who had been assigned to the expedition for just such a contact. McClure wanted to find out if the Inuit had knowledge of the fate of Franklin and his crew. He also hoped to gain geographical knowledge of the region. It was not known at the time if Prince Albert Land (located north of Minto Inlet), Wollaston Land (located south of Prince Albert Sound), and Victoria Land (located in southeast Victoria Island) were part of the American continent or if they were islands. (Later, of

---

in Barrow Strait, some six hundred miles northeast of the modern community of Holman. Inglefield's 1854 voyage returned most of the *Investigator's* crew to England after they had abandoned ship, and were rescued by another British naval expedition in June 1853. It is a mystery why Holman Island is named after an assistant surgeon on a supply voyage that did not pass close to the Holman region. Possibly Holman, in his capacity as medical doctor, developed friendships with *Investigator* officers such as McClure and Haswell on the return voyage to England, and that his name was eventually applied to one of the *Investigator's* geographical discoveries. It is also possible that McClure and Haswell were already acquainted with Holman before starting the expedition in 1850. The name Holman Island was officially approved by the government on June 6, 1952. The name of the settlement was officially approved as Holman on March 3, 1960 and confirmed on March 9, 1979. Holman Island, as the name of the settlement, has never been officially approved (Secretariat of Geographical Names, personal communication, January 9, 1990).

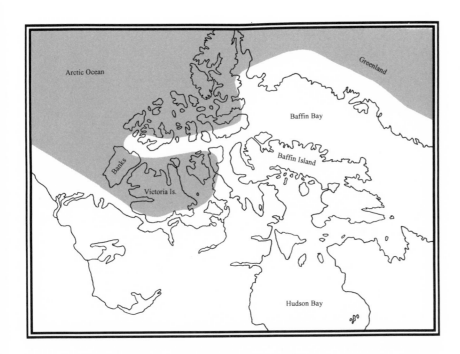

Map 5. European view of the known Arctic, circa 1840. The unshaded areas show the territory that had been explored and mapped by the mid-eighteenth century. Until the midnineteenth century, most of the islands in the Canadian Archipelago remained either undiscovered or incompletely mapped. When English explorer Sir John Franklin left England in 1845 with the ships *Erebus* and *Terror*, it was hoped that he and his men would navigate the Northwest Passage in a single season. After several years, when the Franklin expedition failed to return, rescue parties were sent into the Canadian Archipelago seeking survivors. Between 1848 and 1859, more than fifty expeditions were sent, including the Collinson and McClure expeditions to Victoria Island. These crews sailed and sledged through unexplored portions of the Canadian Arctic, producing better maps of the region. No survivors from the Franklin expedition were ever found. The strip of "known" territory in the center of the map resulted from Lt. William Parry's first expedition (1819–1820). Parry and his crew wintered on Melville Island and made numerous sledge trips, including the first known visit by Europeans to northern Banks Island (map adapted from Berton 1988:335).

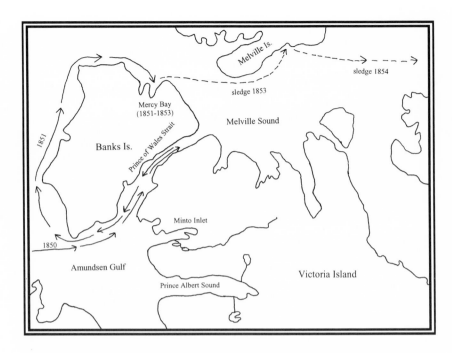

Map 6. Route of the *Investigator* under Robert McClure, 1850 to 1853. McClure wintered in Prince of Wales Strait near the Princess Royal Islands. During the spring of 1851, McClure and his men had repeated contacts with the Copper Inuit of Minto Inlet, making them the first Europeans to meet the northernmost group of Copper Inuit. After rounding Banks Island, the *Investigator* was abandoned in Mercy Bay. The crew cached their remaining supplies on shore. Several years later, this depot was discovered by Copper Inuit from Minto Inlet and Prince Albert Sound and for several decades the Inuit traveled to Mercy Bay to scavenge metal and softwood.

course, it would be determined that these lands all made up a single island—Victoria Island.)

McClure and Miertsching connected with the Inuit group several days later at the same location. Through Miertsching, they informed McClure that they belonged to the neighboring land of Wollaston, meaning, probably, that they were from Prince Albert Sound. They said that they had never seen white men before and that their only communication was with a neighboring tribe, inland, with whom they traded. In all probability, McClure had encountered a group of Kangiryuarmiut (Prince Albert Sound people). These people often traded with their southern neighbors, the Puivlirmiut, during the summers.

As Diamond Jenness later reported in his extensive ethnography of the Copper Inuit, the Prince Albert Sound and Minto Inlet peoples often traveled overland to Lake Tahiryuak (also known as Quunnguq) south of Prince Albert Sound. There they would meet and trade with the Puivlirmiut, who occupied the southern part of Victoria Island.

During McClure's brief meeting with these people, he asked them to draw a map of the coastline. McClure and Miertsching were extremely impressed with the extent and detail of the Inuit's knowledge of the western and southern coasts of the island. The drawing made it clear that Victoria Land, Prince Albert Land, and Wollaston Land were all part of a large island separated from the mainland. By drawing this map for their visitors, the Inuit from Prince Albert Sound filled in a large blank on McClure's maps.

McClure and his men noted that these Inuit made extensive use of copper for making hunting implements and other tools:

> their knives, arrows, needles, and other cutting and piercing instruments were all made of copper—several specimens of which were obtained—fashioned into shape entirely by hammering. No igneous power being had recourse to, it was surprising to see the admirable nature of the work, considering the means by which it was effected, and the form reflected great credit on their ingenuity and excellence in the adaptation of design. (Armstrong 1857:339–340).

Before departing, the British gave the Inuit several presents. McClure took off his thick, red shawl and gave it to a young Inuit woman who was packing a child on her back. The young woman was most embarrassed because she had no item to give to him in return. She took her baby from under her hood and offered it reluctantly to McClure in exchange. Miertsching was able to communicate to the young woman that McClure was not proposing any kind of formal trade with the Inuit but was merely giving gifts for which he expected no compensation (Berton 1988:225). The Inuit were impressed with such generosity and reciprocated with copper tools and skins. One of the expedition members later noted:

> They were quite devoid of all that mercenary spirit, and those strong thieving and other propensities so universal amongst the Esquimaux on the American coast [i.e., North Alaska]—the result of their contact with civilized man—being a few of the evils which invariably follow his footsteps over the world. . . . They

were quite ignorant that there existed any other people differing from themselves in manners and customs; and asked our party where they came from, and where their hunting ground was situated. Their entire occupation consisted of hunting and fishing, migrating to and from along this coast, fixing their temporary abode wherever success was most likely to attend their efforts; and appeared to be influenced by no other feeling than the acquisition of what was essential to their sustenance from one season to another, to afford them sufficient food and raiment for sustaining life and protecting them from the cold (Armstrong 1857:340).

The meeting—the first European contact and communication with this northernmost group of Copper Inuit—was brief. But from their written observations, it is clear that these explorers were extremely impressed with the Inuit's remarkable ability to survive in such a harsh climate, using ingenious tools and hunting implements made from the limited resources at their disposal. Since no trade items of southern manufacture had yet reached this isolated region of the Arctic, these people were totally independent and self-reliant.

With spring break-up, the *Investigator* again attempted to travel north through Prince of Wales Strait, seeking to reach Melville Sound. The attempt was in vain. The ship was stopped by ice. McClure, desperately wanting to reach Melville Sound that summer and thus be the first to navigate the Northwest Passage, decided instead to turn the *Investigator* around and sail up the treacherous west coast of Banks Island. The *Investigator* sailed south to Nelson Head, up the west coast, and then east along the north coast of Banks Island. At several points, the ship was in great danger when the permanent pack ice came within inches of crushing the ship against the precipitous cliffs of the north coast. In time, the *Investigator* arrived at a protective bay within which it could escape the encroaching ice pack. The expedition named this protective haven the Bay of God's Mercy and later it became known as Mercy Bay. By this time, the fall season was fairly advanced and there was little possibility of continuing on into Melville Sound. McClure and his men settled down to a second winter in the Arctic. The next spring, however, the ice did not leave the bay and the *Investigator* was forced to spend a third winter locked in. On June 3, 1853, McClure and his crew abandoned the *Investigator* and walked over the ice to Melville Island where they were rescued by another exploration vessel. When the expedition eventually returned to England, McClure and his men were recognized as

Fig. 2.2. The *Investigator* locked in the ice of Mercy Bay, Banks Island. The drawing, by Lt. S. G. Cresswell, shows a sledging party departing from Dealy Island on April 15, 1853. Courtesy of the Royal Ontario Museum, Toronto, Canada.

the first Europeans known to have successfully negotiated the Northwest Passage, albeit not on the same ship—or even traveling all the way by ship at all.

Before abandoning ship, McClure deposited supplies and equipment on the shore. Records compiled by Cliff Hickey (1984:23) from parliamentary sources indicate a great quantity of goods was left behind. It included 3,720 lbs. of salt pork, 12,828 lbs. of flour, 6,388 lbs. of canned meat, 1,234 lbs. of tobacco, 52 gallons of rum, 7 fully equipped whaleboats, 100 empty casks, woodworking tools, sails, clothing, and textiles. This treasure trove on the northern shore of Banks Island had a significant impact upon the Copper Inuit of western Victoria Island, although it is not known how or when this material was discovered by the local people. The Berkeley Point group that McClure had contacted knew that McClure and his men had come from the north, where the *Investigator* had wintered in

1850/1851. Possibly a group of Copper Inuit wanted to trade with McClure and so, headed north looking for him. Or perhaps a group of Inuit discovered the Mercy Bay depot while hunting.

Interviews conducted by the explorer Vilhjalmur Stefansson in 1911 indicate that the Copper Inuit of western Victoria Island probably discovered the icebound *Investigator* and the depot of supplies several years later, around 1855 (Stefansson 1921:360).

Mercy Bay

Albert Palvik. I remember stories that other people from around here would go up there [Mercy Bay] to get things from the ship-wreck, even food like biscuits that were lying around. I don't remember how people got the word to go up there. Hologak used to talk about it. He remembered going up there with the older people when he was a young man. They found a lot of stuff up there that had drifted up on shore, like wood planks.

News of the *Investigator* and the goods deposited on the shore quickly spread throughout Copper Inuit territory—as far south as Coronation Gulf and as far east as King William Island (Stefansson 1921:240). Copper Inuit traveled great distances in order to help themselves to the materials. Much of the material left behind, such as the food and clothing, was of little use to the Inuit. Two items, however, were of immeasurable value: iron and softwood. Stefansson wrote:

> I was surprised when my informants made this distinction between the soft and the hard wood. They explained that the hard wood was almost as difficult to make anything out of as caribou antlers and not nearly so durable. In other words, they saw no use for hard wood except to replace bone or horn, and bone or horn was better than hard wood. But the soft wood was a superior variety of the driftwood which they were familiar with and very useful. What they did was to take the barrels, no matter what they contained, and break them up with the object of using the hoops. The staves being of hard wood were no more valuable than the food or rum contained in the barrels. Similarly, boxes containing clothing were opened, the clothes thrown away and the boxes made into arrow shafts and the like. (Stefansson 1921:360)

At some point, the *Investigator* either drifted away or sank. Stefansson states that his older informants, interviewed in 1911, did not know what exactly had happened to the ship. One year, the ship had been grounded on the beach; the next year it was gone without a trace.

For almost the next half century, Copper Inuit from Victoria Island made periodic trips to Mercy Bay. Stefansson estimated that this salvaging of shore cache lasted until about 1890 when depletion of game may have forced people back to their usual territories, namely western Victoria Island and southeastern Banks Island (Hickey 1984:19). The salvaged materials from the *Investigator*, the first nonindigenous items to be introduced into the economy, eventually spread throughout the northern Copper Inuit population. Even today, archaeological sites in Prince Albert Sound yield evidence of iron and wood originally carried north by the McClure expedition, one example being the Kunana site in Prince Albert Sound, described in chapter 1. Although McClure and his crew had only fleeting contact with the Copper Inuit of western Victoria Island, the impact they had on the local economy was profound.

A year after McClure and his crew spent their first winter in Prince of Wales Strait (1850/1851), another British naval vessel entered the territory of the Copper Inuit. This was the *Enterprise*, under the command of Richard Collinson—part of the same expedition as the *Investigator*. The ships had become separated while rounding Cape Horn on the southern tip of South America. Collinson had hoped to catch up with McClure, but was never able to do so.[2] Instead, Collinson changed course and spent the winter of 1850/1851 in Hong Kong. Returning to the

2. The two ships had actually become separated in mist and fog while going through the Straits of Magellan at the southern tip of South America. McClure and his superior, Collinson, had arranged to rendezvous at Cape Lisburne, Alaska. When McClure reached Honolulu to take on fresh water and supplies, he learned that Collinson had waited several days for him but departed for Alaska the previous morning. After hurriedly resupplying his ship, in just three days, McClure set off to catch up with Collinson's vessel. In his effort to make it to the rendezvous point before Collinson, McClure decided to cut straight through the foggy and unchartered Aleutian Island chain rather than go around its western terminus, as Collinson was doing. Even though McClure was supposed to wait for his superior at Cape Lisburne, he forged ahead, passing Cape Barrow and entering the Beaufort Sea. When Collinson arrived off the coast of Alaska, he learned of McClure's bold departure into unknown seas. Collinson cautiously turned his ship around and retreated to Hong Kong for the winter (see Berton 1988:296–299).

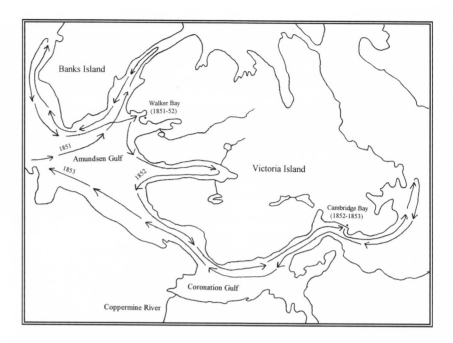

Map 7. Route of the *Enterprise* under Richard Collinson, 1851 to 1853. After exploring the southern coast of Banks Island, the *Enterprise* wintered in Walker Bay. During the spring, while mapping the coastline, Collinson and his men had repeated contacts with the Copper Inuit of Minto Inlet and Walker Bay. In the summer of 1852, the *Enterprise* explored Prince Albert Sound and the southern coast of Victoria Island. After wintering in Cambridge Bay, in 1852/1853 the *Enterprise* headed back toward Alaska.

Arctic in the summer of 1851, Collinson had hoped to discover McClure's whereabouts and reunite the expedition under a single command (his own). Collinson found a safe habor in Walker Bay and there spent the winter of 1851/1852. The name Fort Collinson, the site where they wintered, still appears on modern maps. A number of sledging expeditions were sent out during the winter, but Collinson did not know that McClure and his men were wintering a good distance away, approximately 150 miles to the northwest at Mercy Bay. Collinson had fleeting contacts with the Inuit of Minto Inlet. One person to visit Collinson's ship that winter was an Inuk named Pammiungittok, who was then about eight years old. Pammiungittok, interviewed by Stefansson sixty years later, was the only one still alive who remembered seeing Collinson. According to Pammiungittok, Collinson and his men "were excellent people who paid well for water boots," and that they "threw away much valuable stuff which the people picked up" (Stefansson 1913:287).

Like McClure the year before, Collinson sent out spring sledging parties to explore and map the coastline of Victoria Island. One such group, under the command of a Lieutenant Jago, headed across the mouth of Minto Inlet and into Prince Albert Sound. Jago's journal provides, in some detail, a description of Holman Island, discovered the year before by Haswell of the *Investigator*. Jago's party continued down Prince Albert Sound, traveling between the coast and a large number of islands. At one point, Jago traversed an island with a cairn on it. Inside the cairn was the cylinder containing a message written the year before by Haswell's sledging expedition. Jago continued deeper into Prince Albert Sound, where he encountered a party of Inuit camped on the ice. The meeting was friendly. As Jago states in his journal: "I purchased two dogs of them, also some reindeer's meat, and fish, and when I made signs to them that we were going to sleep, they perfectly understood me, and we parted very good friends. One of the dogs made his escape during the night" (quoted in Collinson 1889:206).

The following day, Jago met another, larger group of Inuit—forty-five men and two women. Jago states that these people "wanted us very much to come up to their encampment," but since Jago had left a number of ill men behind at his last camp, he decided it best to return without visiting the Inuit camp. Before heading back, Jago erected a cairn and placed a message in it. This marked the easternmost point of his expedition. According to his journal, this furthest point was latitude 70°34' north and longitude 110°15' west. These figures, however, must be mistaken because they would have placed Jago well inland from the eastern end of Prince Albert Sound.

Jago returned to the ship at Walker Bay, retracing his steps out of Prince Albert Sound and across Minto Inlet. In his report to Collinson, he states: "The places that I have named beyond the *Investigator's* beacon [i.e., beyond the point where Haswell had turned back], I hope you will let remain, and that what I have done will meet with your approbation" (quoted in Collinson 1889:207). How far Jago penetrated into Prince Albert Sound it is impossible to determine, but he must certainly have gone deeper than did the previous year's expedition under Haswell.

Although Collinson and his men had only fleeting contacts

with the Inuit, they provided Europe with the earliest visual images of the northernmost Copper Inuit. This was a time before photographic equipment was taken on exploration vessels and all visual records of northern expeditions had to be drawn by hand. The assistant surgeon of the *Enterprise*, Edward Adams, an amateur artist, made a number of sketches and paintings of the Inuit. The sketches were probably made during the winter of 1851/1852, when the *Enterprise* was in Walker Bay. They are remarkably accurate, displaying the skin clothing and facial tattooing typical of the Copper Inuit. Not until 1911 were more

Fig. 2.3. Watercolor drawing of Copper Inuit family by Edward Adams, assistant surgeon on the *Enterprise*. This drawing was probably made during the winter of 1851/1852 when the *Enterprise* was wintering in Walker Bay. Expedition records mention meeting a group of Copper Inuit fishing in the lakes inland from the bay. This drawing and the one following represent the first visual record of the Copper Inuit of northwestern Victoria Island. Courtesy of the archives of the Scott Polar Research Institute.

34

Fig. 2.4. Watercolor drawing of Copper Inuit man with a loon dancing hat, northwestern Victoria Island. Drawing by Edward Adams, 1851 to 1852. Courtesy of the archives of the Scott Polar Research Institute.

images of the region's Inuit made. By then, it was using photographic technology.

In the summer of 1852, Collinson left Walker Bay and explored the north and south shores of Prince Albert Sound. The *Enterprise* spent the next winter (1852/1853) in Cambridge Bay, where further exploration took place. In the summer of 1853, the *Enterprise* headed back to England by retracing its route via North Alaska and Cafe Horn.

Klengenberg of the Arctic

After the departure of McClure and Collinson, the Holman region was undisturbed by outside exploration for over half a century. Inuit groups to both the east and west were beset by commercial whalers, but the regions of the Central Arctic were too isolated and inaccessible to offer encouragement to such activity. Moreover, there was an ice cover during most of the year and large bowhead whales rarely ventured deep into the Canadian Archipelago.

In 1906, the Canadian government issued a map of the Canadian Arctic, marking Victoria Island as uninhabited. It was believed at the time that the Inuit encountered by Collinson and McClure fifty years earlier had migrated to the west coast of Hudson Bay in order to trade with whalers. Ottawa did not know that in the same year the map was issued, an independent trader named Christian Klengenberg had landed on Victoria Island and made contact with a large group of Copper Inuit.

Christian Klengenberg was a Dane, born in 1869 at Svendborg, a small town on the south coast of the Danish island of Funen. Even in his teens, Klengenberg displayed the roaming spirit that would characterize his exploits for the rest of his life. In 1885, at the age of sixteen, Klengenberg signed on as an assistant cook aboard a Danish ship traveling from Copenhagen to New York City. During the next few years, Klengenberg worked on a number of ships, sailing to Shanghai, Africa, Alaska, Australia, and many other places. In 1893, he sailed on the *Emily Schroeder*, which traveled through the Bering Strait to the Inupiat (North Alaskan) community of Point Hope (Tikigaq). The purpose of the expedition was to trade with the Inupiat along the North Alaskan coast. Members of the expedition built a small trading post near the community of Point Hope and settled down for the long arctic winter. It was Klengenberg's first exposure to the Arctic and it is apparent in his autobiography that he relished the northern life. During the winter of 1893/1894, Klengenberg spent most of his time with the young Inupiat men from the village, whose company he preferred "over the dull adults for whom I cooked at the trading post" (Klengenberg 1932:90). Klengenberg also courted and eventually married a young Inupiat woman, Gremnia (Qimniq), with whom he had eight children.

In the spring of 1894, Klengenberg took temporary leave of his young wife and traveled to Herschel Island aboard the steam-driven whaler *Orka*. Although Klengenberg had not traveled more than two to three miles on the ice outside of Point Hope, he convinced the *Okra*'s captain that he had intimate knowledge of the North Alaskan coastline and the skipper hired him as the ship's pilot. Fortunately, the trip from Point Hope to Herschel Island was made without incident.

By the 1890s, Herschel Island had become a bustling whaling center for the western Canadian Arctic. Located between the Mackenzie Delta and the Alaska-Canada border, Herschel was a major trading post and winter harbor for whalers. In summertime, the boats plied the Beaufort Sea hunting bowheads. Klengenberg had planned to return immediately to Point Hope, but he could not resist the temptation of signing on as a whaler aboard the *Mary D. Hume*. He thus spent the summer whaling in the Beaufort Sea. At one point, the ship anchored off Banks Island to take on fresh meat and Klengenberg was among those who disembarked. While walking on the tundra, he spotted footprints and concluded they had been made the same summer. Klengenberg was excited at the possibility that there were unknown bands of Inuit on Banks Island. Reflecting upon this discovery many years later, Klengenberg wrote: "If a trader could get into their country with a good supply of trade goods, he might have a chance to get furs cheaper than elsewhere in the Arctic, and could become wealthy" (Klengenberg 1932:128).

Realizing the significance of his observation, Klengenberg did not mention the footprints to any of his fellow crew members. It was not until nine years later, in 1905, that he had an opportunity to travel to Victoria Island to seek the unknown group of Inuit that he was sure must reside there. Captain Charles McKenna, an arctic whaler turned trader with the collapse of the commercial whaling industry, offered to put Klengenberg in charge of a schooner, the *Olga*, which McKenna had generously loaded down with trade goods. McKenna had originally approved of Klengenberg's plan to seek out the Inuit of Victoria Island, but he changed his mind at the last minute and instructed Klengenberg to take the *Olga* from Baillie Island to Herschel Island. On the way to Herschel Island, the *Olga* was conveniently pushed eastward by a gale, a development that pleased Klengenberg, who did nothing to prevent the schooner from being blown far off course.[3] The *Olga* made landfall on the west coast of Wollaston Peninsula, Victoria Island. There,

---

3. There is disagreement regarding the circumstances of this event. Klengenberg claimed that he was legitimately blown off course, but some of his detractors claimed that he intentionally took the ship eastward, using the gale as an excuse for making landfall on Victoria Island. The truth may lie somewhere in between.

at a location now named Penny Bay, Klengenberg set up winter
quarters. In addition to his crew and three western Inuit families, Klengenberg was accompanied by his wife, Gremnia, and
three children, a son Patsy and daughters Weena and Lena.
A second son was born during the winter and named after
Klengenberg's father, Jorgen.

For much of the winter, Klengenberg had difficulty dealing
with his crew, many of whom were bored and disgruntled at
being forced to spend the winter at such an isolated spot. Four
men died over the course of the winter—two when they fell

Fig. 2.5. Klengenberg family at Baillie Island, July 26, 1916. From
left to right, Etna, Jorgen, Gremnia (Qimniq) with Bob in her arms,
Patsy, Andrew, Captain Christian (Charlie) Klengenberg, and Lena
(daughter Weena not shown). The photo was taken soon after son Patsy
had completed the winter working as an assistant to anthropologist
Diamond Jenness. Klengenberg had left Patsy with Jenness at Bernard
Harbour, to work in exchange for being taught to read and write.
When Patsy was returned to his family, Klengenberg was so grateful
that he gave Jenness one blue and two white fox skins (Jenness 1991:
619–20). Photo by Diamond Jenness. Courtesy of the Canadian Museum of Civilization, No. 36912.

through thin ice, another of natural causes, and the fourth (the ship's mechanic) was killed by Klengenberg in self-defense. Klengenberg's autobiography (1932) provides Klengenberg's version of these events.

Westerners and Kangiryuarmiut

Frank Kuptana. Long ago, the westerners and Kangiryuarmiut would meet one another. When the Kangiryuarmiut were out polar bear hunting, they would come upon the westerners using matches and smoking their pipes. The Kangiryuarmiut would run away, afraid of the Westerners because of their matches. Maybe that's how they started fighting. The Kangiryuarmiut didn't know about matches and pipes back then. The westerners say that they thought the Kangiryaurmiut would be thirsty from all their traveling and would call them back to have water because it was ready. But they just kept running away. On some occasions, when the westerners had their rifles, they would shoot at the Kangiryuarmiut while they were running away. The Kangiryuar-miut and westerners didn't know that each other were real. The Kangiryuarmiut didn't know about pipes and matches. That's why they would run away. The Kangiryuarmiut had only bows, arrows, and harpoons, while the westerners had rifles.

   The Western Inuit who had accompanied Klengenberg on the *Olga* set up trapping camps at some distance from the ship. One day, while checking their snares, they encountered a group of Kangiryuarmiut (Prince Albert Sound people):

> Kromanak, Tadjuk, and their wives had been visiting their snares when three Eskimo strangers came to their tents. They had come on foot. While they were talking, Kromanak, who felt like smok-ing, filled his pipe with tobacco, took out a match and lit his pipe—and the three visitors cleared out as fast as they could [frightened by the magical power]. . . . As they fled, Kromanak and Tadjuk had a good time firing shots close to them to make them go faster! (Metayer 1966:41–42).

The western Inuit Kromanak and Tadjuk related this story to another westerner, Nuligak, on their return to Herschel Island the following year. Nuligak eventually mentions this story in his biography, edited by Father Maurice Metayer. In the book,

I, Nuligak, Kromanak and Tadjuk offer no explanation for their seemingly hostile behavior to the Kangiryuarmiut. They report, however, being approached and surrounded sometime later by a group of these Inuit brandishing knives:

> And those Krangmalit[4] visitors had put them [Kromanak and Tadjuk] through close questioning: "Why had they opened fire on them?" "Where in the world did they come from, to act as though they were dangerous men?" Kromanak and Tadjuk answered that their country was named Abvak: they had come from Cape Bathurst. The Krangmalit then said, "In that case you are related to us, for our ancestors originated there—then why be enemies?" After this statement, the old Krangmalit left the tent and called loudly to their kinsmen to come. A great number of sleds appeared from their hiding place behind a point of land. In those days many Inuit lived around the Prince Albert Sound (Metayer 1966:42).

When Kromanak and Tadjuk informed Klengenberg of their encounter with this new group of Inuit, Klengenberg loaded up one of his sleds with trade goods and headed northward along the coast accompanied by a handful of western Inuit. After three days, Klengenberg and his companions reached Cape Baring on the eastern tip of Wollaston Peninsula, just south of Prince Albert Sound. Rounding the bluff of Cape Baring, Klengenberg spotting a large group of Inuit:

4. According to Metayer (1966:41), the term *Krangmalit* was used by the westerners (primarily people from the Mackenzie Delta) to describe the Inuit of the central Arctic, including the Kangiryuarmiut and other Copper Inuit groups. It is widely used even today and basically means "people to the east." A more accurate spelling of the term using the ILC orthography is probably *Qangmalit*. While the origin of the term is unclear, de Coccala and King (1986:328) state that it derives from the word *kranga* (or *qanga*), meaning "beyond". This seems unlikely, since none of our informants (even those from the west) had ever heard of this usage. A more reasonable explanation is that Qangmalit derives from the term *qangmaq*, which refers to the banking, or berming, around the base of a snowhouse (not to be confused with *qanmaq*, which refers to calling a dog). According to Father Tardy (personal communication), the banking of snowhouses was a common practice in the Copper Inuit region, at least in comparison with the western Arctic, so the term became a way to distinguish western Inuit from the Copper Inuit to the east (literally: "people who bank their snowhouses"). Metayer (1966:41) also claims that the term could be used in a slightly pejorative sense by westerners, who felt that the Krangmalit (or Qangmalit) were relatively primitive. A number of the western Inuit living in Holman deny this and claim that the term is no more pejorative than the designation Walliningmiut. The term is rather archaic and appears only rarely in historical documents.

Men, women, and children—all were dressed in clothes of caribou skin, but cut after a fashion differing a bit from any which I had seen before. The skins had been tanned, as usual, with head and ears attached, so as to have hoods like those on a parka or cowl on a monk's robe. The men held copper snow-knives aloft in both hands, and kept thrusting them straight up and down above their heads. Incredible as it may seem, they did not stop their dance as they sighted us, but formed into an advancing half-moon, as if to encircle us, and this they did without a break.... I afterwards learned that this was a friendly manner of approach (Klengenberg (1932:226).

The Inuit who had accompanied Klengenberg, however, were frightened by this display of goodwill and ran away. Klengenberg rose from his sled as he was surrounded by the large group of Inuit. Klengenberg reports that one old woman came close to him and started hopping around him in a funny manner. She told the rest to stand back since this man was a dangerous person. Klengenberg's response to this accusation was a novel one:

Hearing that, I lifted both my hands high in the air and laughed, and then, just as the old woman was near me I suddenly grabbed her around the waist, and said something in Eskimo which is the equivalent of asking for a kiss, and I drew her close and rubbed noses with her. . . . At that, the entire crowd began to laugh like children, and the old woman herself laughed and seemed quite pleased. They saw that I had no weapon on me, not even a knife. I began to talk as well as I could in Eskimo, and I saw that they understood most of what I was saying. I pointed to the south, telling them I was a man from very far away who had come to make trade with them (Klengenberg 1932:226).

The western Inuit who had accompanied Klengenberg eventually overcame their fright and drew nearer. They were able to communicate better than Klengenberg who he was and what he wanted. Klengenberg noted that all of their tools were made from native copper. Only one man had a knife made from the blade of a handsaw. The man could not say where he had gotten the knife, only that it had been handed down from father to son for many generations. This knife may have been made from a sawblade salvaged many years before from the *Investigator*'s depot at Mercy Bay.

The Inuit were anxious to obtain the wares that Klengenberg

had packed on his sled and he began trading with them. Although they had no raw furs to trade, Klengenberg took from them soapstone pots, copper snowknives, and the fur garments that they were wearing. Then a celebration was held, with dancing, eating, and singing. Before the two groups departed in different directions,

> the head man of the new people told me to get more iron and knives and then to come to their settlements in the interior. He gave me directions by which I might find them. He said that he would see to it that next time I would be able to get plenty of furs without taking their pants away from them. Then we all laughed and said good things, and the new people went their way towards the interior and we went our way back to the ship (Klengenberg 1932:229).

Later that winter, Klengenberg loaded another sled with trade goods and left to find the Inuit camp, taking with him his eldest daughter Weena, who had just turned twelve. After several days of traveling, they located and entered a camp made up of over thirty snowhouses. Klengenberg spent the next three days trading with the people, but barely escaped with his life when an informant told him of a plot to murder him and take the steel runners of his sled. In his biography, Klengenberg relates how he made his escape by calling together all the members of the community and tossing to the crowd the remainder of his trade goods. In the ensuing free-for-all, Klengenberg and his daughter were able to ready their sled and make their departure.

The next summer, Klengenberg returned to Herschel Island and resigned as the captain of the *Olga*. Klengenberg's reappearance with the *Olga* caused much excitement and controversy. Captain McKenna, her owner, was furious that Klengenberg had taken the ship to Victoria Island without his permission, in spite of Klengenberg's claim that he was blown off course. There was also speculation concerning the circumstances surrounding the deaths of the four crewmen. Klengenberg was eventually tried on two separate occasions for the murder of the mechanic (once by Canadian authorities and again by U.S. authorities) and acquitted in both cases.

During the next few years, Klengenberg occupied himself with a variety of activities, hunting, trapping, whaling, and trading throughout North Alaska and the western Canadian

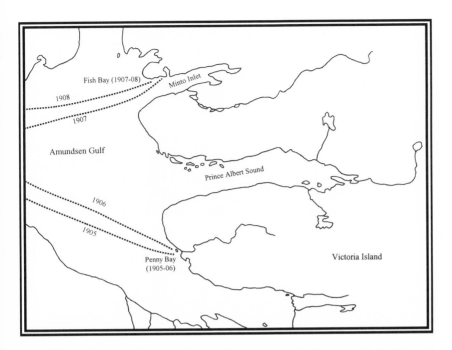

Map 8. Wintering locations of the *Olga*—1905/1906 under Christian
Klengenberg and 1907/1908 under William Mogg. Klengenberg was
the first European to visit the Copper Inuit of Prince Albert Sound
after McClure's and Collinson's expeditions in the mid-1850s. In the
same year that Klengenberg contacted the Inuit people, the Canadian
government issued a map that marked Victoria Island as uninhabited.
It was believed that the Copper Inuit seen by McClure and Collinson
in the 1850s had migrated to western Hudson Bay in order to trade
with commercial whalers. After Klengenberg's contact, traders entered the region in droves.

Arctic. Not until 1916 was he able to return to the Coronation
Gulf area and set up a temporary trading post. This was near
Cape Kendall, to the north of Coppermine. Klengenberg moved
several times before establishing a permanent trading post at
Rymer Point, on the southwest coast of Victoria Island, in 1919.
Klengenberg and his family settled into the new quarters at
Rymer Point. Most of Klengenberg's children, both males and
females, became active traders in the region. His daughter Etna
(Edna) and her husband, Ikey Bolt, an Inuk from the western
Arctic, eventually took over Klengenberg's store at Rymer
Point.

Ikey Bolt

Albert Palvik. I remember Ikey Bolt as a hunter and trapper down around the end of Prince Albert Sound—Halahiqvik and Kayalihuk. We used to travel a lot with Malgokak. Malgokak was orphaned when he was a young man and Ikey took him in. Malgokak was a young man just beginning to learn how to hunt when his parents died. His father was Kitekudlak. Ikey then adopted him. Sometimes they traveled up to Minto and Kuujuak too. From their trapping, they were able to buy a boat. They traveled to Coppermine, but they never really traveled with their schooner around here. Malgokak married a woman from down there, but she died. He moved back here and married Elsie Alikamek.

Sam Oliktoak. I never met Charlie [Klengenberg], but I met his sons-in-law, Ikey Bolt and George Avakana. My parents used to trade with Avakana at Cape Krusenstern and later traded with Ikey Bolt at Rymer Point. Charlie would bring supplies on his ship to Ikey's post at Rymer Point and to George Avakana's post at Cape Krusenstern.

Ruth Nigiyonak. Ikey Bolt was married to Etna [Klengenberg] and had his own store at a place called Nuvuk or Rymer Point. There were people who lived there all year round. The father of Patsy and Jorgen was Charlie Klengenberg, known as Charliuyak. Charlie Klengenberg came to Rymer Point by boat. He was a white man. He had a big boat. His wife always stayed behind when he went places. She stayed with her family. Charlie and his wife had quite a few children. After they stopped having children, Charlie started to travel more often. Then they were separated and most likely divorced. Charlie's wife's name was Qimniq. She stayed and lived with her children since the eldest [Patsy] was doing very well hunting and living off the land.

Another daughter, Lena, and her husband, George Avakana, set up a trading post at Cape Krusenstern that operated from 1926 to 1936. Klengenberg's first born son, Patsy, also became a trader in the Coronation Gulf region until his untimely death from a fire aboard his schooner, the *Aklavik* (see Webster 1980:101). Many of Klengenberg's descendants currently live in the communities of Holman and Coppermine.

Several years after Klengenberg's visit with the Inuit of Prince Albert Sound, whaling captain William Mogg spent the winter in a small bay on the northern side of Minto Inlet. On contemporary maps, this small bay is called Fish Bay, a little to the west of Omingmagiuk (known on maps as Boot Inlet). Mogg had more than twenty years of experience in arctic whaling; and like many captains in the western Arctic he turned to trading with the collapse of commercial whaling at the turn of the century. Mogg loaded a ship with trade goods and spent the winter of 1907/1908 in Minto Inlet. Mogg's ship was the *Olga*, the same ship captained by Klengenberg two years earlier.

There is no written documentation or ship's log providing details of this trading expedition: perhaps it was the news of Klengenberg's contact with the Prince Albert Sound people that stimulated Mogg's trip to Minto. What information is available concerning Mogg's visit comes from interviews with Holman elders. Nicholas Uluariuk states that his father, Mark Emerak, visited Mogg's ship while very young. Since Emerak was only six or seven years old at the time, his recollections may be based more upon the stories told him by older people who visited the ship than upon personal memory. In any event, according to Uluariuk, this was the first ship and the first group of white people that Emerak could remember seeing. A print made by Emerak many years later shows Mogg's ship as he remembered it. In recollections told to his children, Emerak said a group of Inuit had boarded the ship, getting away with a supply of guns and ammunition while Mogg and his crew were camped on the shore. Emerak did not indicate if there were any reprisals for this incident.

Mogg was interested in exploring the Kuujjuak River for evidence of native copper, which Klengenberg had reported to be in great abundance on Victoria Island. According to Holman elder Uluariuk, Mogg, or one of his men, accompanied an Inuk named Taptualuk up the river, but found no evidence of copper. Upon their return, Taptualuk was given some rifles, ammunition, and a bag of flour. Since the Copper Inuit at the time had no use, or taste, for southern food, the flour was dumped on the ground so that the bag could be used as a container (Uluariuk interview, June 8, 1989). If the story is accurate, Taptualuk was one of the first Inuit in the Holman region to receive a firearm.

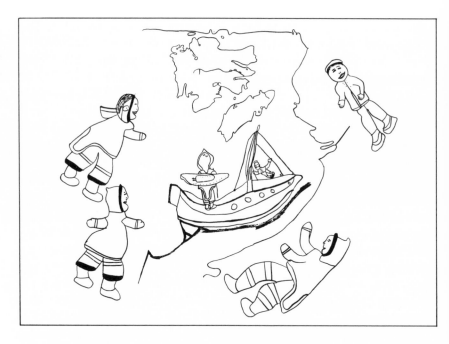

Fig. 2.6. *First White Man's Ship.* Lithograph drawing by Holman elder and artist Mark Emerak. The ship in the drawing is probably the *Olga*, which wintered at Fish Bay in 1907/1908. This was the first white man's ship that Emerak—a child of six or seven at the time the Copper Inuit visited the ship remembers seeing. The ship, under the command of Captain Mogg, went to Minto Inlet to trade with the Inuit. Courtesy of the Holman Eskimo Cooperative.

Vilhjalmur Stefansson and the Canadian Arctic Expedition

Until the first decade of the twentieth century, contact with the Inuit of western Victoria Island and eastern Banks Island was sporadic. McClure, Collinson, Klengenberg, and Mogg offer little detailed information concerning the culture, population, or movements of the people they met. The published works of the noted anthropologist and explorer Vilhjalmur Stefansson offer the first detailed information about the Copper Inuit.

Stefansson had been at Herschel Island on his first arctic expedition when Klengenberg returned in 1906 from his trading expedition to Victoria Island. As an anthropologist, Stefansson was most interested in the stories Klengenberg and his crew told about this "new group" of Inuit. Klengenberg reported that

the people dressed in parkas with long tails in the back, that
they used weapons and tools made out of copper, that most of
them had never seen a white man (except for the very oldest,
who reported seeing Collinson in the winter of 1851/1852), and
that Victoria Island abounded in copper. Since Klengenberg
had traded extensively with these Inuit, he was able to show
Stefansson and others his collection of Kangiryuarmiut knives
hammered out of native copper, finely made bows with sinew
backing, quivers full of arrows tipped with copper, and dozens
of suits of clothing expertly sewn with copper needles (Stefansson 1906). Klengenberg and his crew also reported that some
of the Prince Albert Sound people looked much like Europeans,
having light hair color and blue or gray eyes (Usher 1965:47;
Stefansson 1928:191). The western Inuit who had accompanied
Klengenberg confirmed this observation of so-called blond Inuit. Two years later, even Captain Mogg returned with similar
reports of blond Inuit based upon his contact with people in
Minto Inlet.

As a result of these intriguing reports, Stefansson decided to
see these people for himself. During his second expedition to
the Arctic (1908 to 1912), under the auspices of the American
Museum of Natural History, he traveled extensively in Copper
Inuit territory. Accompanying him was an Inuk from Port Clarence, Alaska, named Natkusiak (also known as Billy Banksland),
who would be Stefansson's primary traveling companion and
guide until the end of Stefansson's third Arctic expedition
(1918). Natkusiak, who shared Stefansson's enthusiasm for Arctic travel and exploration, later settled down in the Holman
region and raised a family.

In 1910, Stefansson and Natkusiak spent the summer exploring the region between Coronation Gulf and Great Bear Lake.
The following spring, the two men, traveling by dogsled,
reached Prince Albert Sound and made contact with the Copper
Inuit who had met with Klengenberg several years before. In
his book *My Life with the Eskimo* (1913), Stefansson writes of
having arrived at a small island near the south shore of Prince
Albert Sound:

From the top of the island the next morning I could with the
glasses see a native village on the ice ten or fifteen miles to the
northwest, approximately in the middle of Prince Albert Sound.
When we approached it we saw this to be the largest village of
our whole experience. It turned out that there were twenty-seven
dwelling houses in it. We had, of course, seen the ruined trading

47

Fig. 2.7. Copper Inuit women, probably from Prince Albert Sound, circa 1911. Photo by V. Stefansson. Courtesy of the Dartmouth College Library, Stefansson Collection, Lantern slide No. 170.

village at Cape Bexley [on the southern shore of Dolphin and Union Strait], which had over fifty dwellings, but these had been the houses of traders from half a dozen or more different tribes, while this turned out to be the one tribe of the Kanghirgyuarg-miut, and they were not all at home either, for later on we visited another village of three houses of the same people, and a third village of four houses we never saw at all (Stefansson (1913:278).

Stefansson and Natkusiak approached the village and were met several miles south of it by a group of three hunters who had been seal hunting on the ice. The three hunters seemed a little timid at first, but indicated that Stefansson and Natkusiak were welcome in the village. They showed surprise, however, that Stefansson and Natkusiak had come from the southeast, a country inhabited by their neighbors, the Puivlirmiut, "who were now and then in the habit of arriving by the same route as ours, and at this season of the year, for purposes of trade" (Stefansson 1913:279). Stefansson and Natkusiak assured them that they had originated from the southwest but were arriving from the southeast simply because they had been visiting the Hanerag-miut to the south. Stefansson added that they belonged to the same group of people who had visited several years before in

a large schooner—the *Olga*. The three hunters remembered the
Olga and had liked its crew.[5]

First White Men

William Kuptana. The first encounter with white men was at
Kangiqyuak [Prince Albert Sound]. . . . That was the first time they
ever saw white people. The white people were Billy Banksland
[Natkusiak—actually an Inuk from Alaska] and his partner.* That
was also the first time the rifle was introduced to the Inuit. He
[Billy Banksland] advised the Inuit that the gun was dangerous.
He told the Inuit not to handle the rifles.

Incidentally, the herd of caribou were crossing from Banks
Island to Victoria Island near the settlement where the Inuit were
camped. Billy Banksland's partner ran forward to intercept the
herd. He then abruptly aimed and fired the rifle and struck down
one caribou. At that instance, the Inuit immediately rushed to

5. The statement made by the three hunters that they had liked the *Olga*'s
crew may seem odd, given Klengenberg's report that the same people attempted to kill him. This is an example of the kinds of inconsistencies that
appear in the historical record. It could well be that a single individual (or
a small group) had plotted to kill Klengenberg and his daughter in order to
take his steel sledrunners. The fact that Klengenberg was warned indicates
that some members of the group may have been fond of him and did not
want to see him harmed. It would also have been counterproductive to kill
a man who was in a position to trade valuable items. Another possibility is
that Klengenberg misunderstood and overreacted.

*In this interview, Kuptana may be combining in one episode a number
of different meetings that occurred with members of the Canadian Arctic
Expedition (1913–1918) and the earlier Stefansson-Anderson Expedition
(1908–1912). In Stefansson's report of his first meeting with the Kangiryuarmiut (1911)—when he and Natkusiak were travelling together—there is no
mention of hunting caribou (Stefansson 1913:278–296). Although Stefansson
reports seeing many caribou tracks, he makes no mention of any shooting of
the animals. Kuptana was very young at the time of these initial meetings
and his account is undoubtedly based on what he was told by others rather
than his own observation. It is interesting that Kuptana refers to Natkusiak
as a white man. As discussed in the text, Natkusiak was an Alaskan Inupiat
from Port Clarence, Alaska. His descendants say he actually had a very dark
complexion. The label white man had probably more to do with the goods
he had in his possession and the fact that he was with a white man. The "white
man" may have been Stefansson or one of the other expedition members of
the northern party of the Canadian expedition (if the event occurred in the
1913 to 1918 period). It is also possible that memories of Klengenberg's initial
meeting with the Kangiryuarmiut in 1906 has been combined with Natkusiak
and Stefansson's meeting in 1911.

the caribou that was shot down. In no time at all, the fresh killed carcass was devoured by the Inuit.

The white man started in disbelief at the way the carcass disappeared so swiftly. The reason the Inuit devoured the caribou so quickly was because it was a change in diet. Their main staple food all winter was seal meat.

The Inuit of that area thought the two white men were shamans with great powers. The way they exhibited their firearms and other hunting equipment exemplified to the Inuit that they had great powers, especially when they tried out the telescope. They were wonderstruck. After a while, they became wary and starting talking among themselves about the great powers the white men supposedly possessed. The Inuit concluded that the white men had great powers and considered their equipment as taboo.

Shortly after this event, as described above, a number of expeditions followed thereafter in that same area. The expeditions that arrived would trade for raw fur such as caribou skins and mitts. The Inuit had their first sewing needles arrive on one of those expeditions. The Inuit women had their first real sewing needle that was durable. They were quick to comment how the needle decreased their hardships and increased their efficiency. The needles they used before this period were too flexible and were very inefficient because of their lack of rigidity. [The old] copper needles were very flexible and thus inefficient. . . . From then on, the Inuit started getting more advanced sewing accessories. At the same time as the needles, the snowknife and steel traps were also introduced. The Inuit had to be taught how to use these tools. They would trade two steel traps per person. Snowknives [probably metal] traded for five white fox pelts. Guns traded for ten foxes. My grandfather was the first one in our family to get a rifle.

When Stefansson, Natkusiak, and the three hunters came within half a mile of the settlement, Stefansson observed an interesting form of communication:

When we got within about half a mile of the houses, our companions began to communicate with their fellows in the village by the use of one of the few examples of sign language in existence among these Eskimos. The signs consist of one member of an approaching party running a few yards to one side of the sled and stopping, and then running across the trail until he is as many yards on the other side and stopping again. This is repeated several times and signifies that friendly strangers are approaching. This sort of signaling, they told us, is never done by the strangers themselves, but always by local people who have joined the party of the strangers, just as these three people had joined ours (Stefansson 1913:279).

Stefansson and Natkusiak spent three days in this village, interviewing and recording as much information as possible. Stefansson conducted a census, discovering that the settlement was composed of slightly over 150 persons. By including two smaller neighboring settlements, he estimated the entire Prince Albert Sound group to be approximately 176 strong (Stefansson 1913:290).

Among other things, Stefansson learned that this group of people had just arrived from Banks Island, where they had spent the early winter months at various points between De Salis Bay and Nelson Head. Stefansson's informants claimed that they were the only people who lived on Banks Island and that it was now deserted. The information forced Stefansson to change his plans. He had originally planned to spend the summer on Banks Island, hoping to make contact with Inuit groups residing there. Stefansson's informants told him that they were headed eastward and that most of them planned to ascend the Kagloryuak River (at the east end of Prince Albert Sound), where they would spend the summer hunting caribou and trading with the Ekalluktogmiut. The Ekalluktogmiut (people residing around Cambridge Bay) normally spent the winter hunting seal on Dease Strait (on the southeast portion of Victoria Island), but went up the Ekalluktok River in summer to hunt caribou at the same location as the Prince Albert Sound people. Stefansson also learned that a few families planned to detach themselves from the main group and travel north to hunt between Prince Albert Sound and Minto Inlet. Still others planned to head southeast to meet and trade with the Puivlirmiut at Lake Tahiryuak (Quunnguq).

What most impressed Stefansson about these people was the extent of their travels and knowledge of regions beyond Prince Albert Sound. Evidently, the Inuit of Prince Albert Sound were people who traveled extensively for purposes of hunting and trade. As Stefansson (1913:288) notes:

most years, two or three sleds will detach themselves from the main body in Prince Albert Sound, hurry east ahead of the others up the Kagloryuak River and down the Ekalluktok River to Albert

Fig. 2.8. Group of Copper Inuit in winter clothing, gathered in front of snowhouses. These are possibly Kangiryuarmiut of Prince Albert Sound, circa 1911. Photo by V. Stefansson. Courtesy of the Dartmouth College Library, Stefansson Collection.

> Edward Bay, and thence south across the Straits to the Ahiagmiut, who inhabit the coast in the neighborhood of Ogden Bay, where they abandon their sleds, for summer has overtaken them, and proceed south with pack dogs, the people themselves also carry packs, until they reach the shores of Back River, where the Back River people, known to them as the Haningayogmiut, make rafts of their kayaks and ferry them to the south shore of the stream. Resuming their overland travel, they eventually reach Hanbury's Arkilinik River [Thelon River] in its wooded section, probably early in August. The chief object of this journey has been to get wood and wooden articles of all kinds, which they obtain partly by cutting the trees and shaping the wood to their own desires, and partly by barter in exchange for copper implements and such things from the Eskimo of the Arkilinik, whom they call the Pallirgmiut [possibly referring to the Paallirmiut group of Caribou Inuit].

These journeys were among the most impressive trading expeditions conducted by any Central Arctic Inuit group. Taking perhaps the better part of a year, or longer, the Prince Albert Sound people who embarked upon such expeditions had to travel well over six hundred miles to reach the territory of the Caribou Inuit in the vicinity of the modern settlement of Baker Lake.

During his brief stay in Prince Albert Sound, Stefansson made the acquaintance of an elder named Pammiungittok, who resided in a neighboring snowhouse village. Because of his great age, Pammiungittok provided a wealth of useful information about himself and the Prince Albert Sound people. Pammiungittok (as mentioned earlier in this chapter) was the only person still alive who remembered seeing Collinson at Walker Bay in 1852. This elder told Stefansson at length about his visit to Collinson's ship when he was a boy and about the discovery and plundering of McClure's depot at Mercy Bay.

Like Klengenberg and Mogg, Stefansson and Natkusiak noted that some of the Prince Albert Sound people displayed European-like features, such as gray or blue eyes and red or brown hair. A similar observation was made of more southerly Copper Inuit groups in 1821 by Sir John Franklin, who was the first European to enter the Coronation Gulf Region, as well as by Sir Thomas Simpson in 1838 and 1839. Both of these explorers noted Inuit with features very like those of Europeans—in particular, Scandinavians (Stefansson 1921:471). Because these people were extremely isolated and had not yet had the same degree of contact with whalers as the Inuit farther to the east and west, Stefansson concluded that such features could not have been due to recent European admixture. Stefansson suggested that these traits may have come from the lost colony of Norsemen (Vikings) who settled around A.D. 1000 on the southern and western coasts of Greenland. Although these two colonies died out, Stefansson believed it was possible that some survivors may have intermarried with the Inuit and migrated into Copper Inuit territory (Usher 1965:48). Such speculation made excellent newspaper copy, and the issue was eventually highly publicized in the media, resulting in some acrimonious debate. Subsequent ethnographers who entered the region disagreed with Stefansson's theory and stated that these so-called blond features were due either to genetic accidents or to pathological causes such as snowblindness. These latter views have since prevailed (Usher 1965:48). (See also Stefansson 1928 for a review of this interesting issue.)

Stefansson left the Arctic in 1912, but (as mentioned earlier) returned the following year to start a third expedition, this time sponsored by the Canadian government. The Canadian Arctic Expedition of 1913 to 1918 was one of the largest multidisciplinary expeditions ever undertaken by the Canadian government and included scientists from the fields of anthropology, zoology, botany, geography, geology, mineralogy, and oceanography. The expedition was divided into a southern party, based at Bernard Harbor (west of Coppermine), which was to conduct research in the Coronation Gulf region, and a northern party under the command of Stefansson. The primary base for the northern party was at Cape Kellet, on Banks Island, but a number of secondary wintering bases were established on Victoria Island (Walker Bay and Armstrong Point) and Melville Island.[6] The northern party, which included Stefansson's old traveling companion Natkusiak, was responsible for exploring and collecting scientific data for the regions north of Coronation Gulf.

Explorers Winter at Walker Bay

William Kuptana. When the explorers wintered there [Walker Bay], they built themselves a house made of lumber. They insulated the exterior of the house with caribou hides traded from the local Inuit. For a heating apparatus the explorers used a coal-burning stove. That was the first time the Inuit ever saw a house made of lumber.

The explorers who wintered there were all provisioned with caribou. Occasionally, they would hand out some of their provisions to the Inuit. It was good for the Inuit in more ways than one. Gradually, the Inuit obtained rifles. It brought about a change in lifestyle and therefore provided greater efficiency compared to the bow. In the spring, most of the Inuit of that area would go to Walker Bay (Qikohok). The expedition crew was generous in providing clothing and tools. They would frequent that area until autumn.

During that season, the Inuit stayed where the explorers were stationed. I, William Kuptana, was temporarily traded in for a rifle, ten boxes of shells, one saw, and an ulu. I was sold to the white man and his native wife for the sole purpose of assisting his wife. The white man's name was Bill Seymour. I then moved in with them. When the ice went out, we (the expedition crew) went out caribou hunting across Walker Bay. During that summer, part of the crew from the expedition left, probably to go

6. In the late summer of 1915, one of the expedition's ships, the *Polar Bear*, with Stefansson aboard, attempted to sail up Prince Albert Strait between Victoria Island and Banks Island in order to cross Melville Sound. The goal was to establish winter quarters on Melville Island and use that as a base for exploring northward. The *Polar Bear* ran into thick ice and was frozen in near Armstrong Point, just north of Deans Dundas Bay, on the Victoria Island side. The following year, the *Polar Bear* attempted again to make it through Prince of Wales Strait but was forced to turn back because of ice. The following winter (1916/1917) was spent in winter quarters at Walker Bay.

to Melville Island. Shortly after the departure, only one of the crew who left with the expedition returned on foot. He then told the account of his ordeal. He had been walking for so long that even his face was swollen. He was starving but was fortunate enough to encounter a herd of caribou. So he shot one. On shooting it, he immediately rushed over to the caribou carcass and started to nourish himself fervently from the wound of the animal. From there, he regained enough strength to walk the rest of the way to Walker Bay. They waited for the rest of the crew to return that summer in July. Unfortunately, the crew from that expedition did not return. So, from Walker Bay, they took their schooner, the *Polar Bear*, to Nelson Head Imnaqyuaq. At Nelson Head there were people who had been part of another expedition. They too had a number of their crew missing.*

Early Contact History

During this remarkable expedition, Stefansson traveled throughout the northern regions of Copper Inuit territory, making repeated contact with and studies of the people in Minto Inlet, Prince Albert Sound, and Banks Island. In October 1915, Stefansson and two western Inuit companions departed a temporary hunting camp just north of Deans Dundas Bay in order to contact the Copper Inuit of Minto Inlet. After traveling around Mount Phayre, Stefansson came to a village located in a "deep bight" (possibly Fish Bay or Omingmagiuk):

*While it is true that the *Polar Bear* wintered at Walker Bay in 1916/1917, no lives were lost at that location. In the spring, three men left the ship to map the northern coastline of Victoria Island. Before departure, the three men—Storker Storkerson, Martin Kilian, and G. G. Gumaer—were told by the *Polar Bear*'s captain, Henry Gonzales, that if they did not return by August 1, he would sail without them. The three pressed on with the survey; then Gumaer decided he wanted to return to the ship. By this time, they were on the north coast of the island and the spring thaw was well under way. Alone, it would be a dangerous trip and Storkerson and Kilian gave Gumaer a sled, a dog-team, and strict instructions to keep to the coast. Gumaer, however, decided to walk overland and ended up drowning his dog-team while crossing a river. He made it back to the *Polar Bear* but nearly perished in the process. Storkerson and Kilian continued with the survey and made it back before the *Polar Bear* departed.

The previous winter (December 1916), two men did in fact perish while transporting supplies from Cape Kellett, one of the expedition's bases on southwestern Banks Island, to Melville Island. Both men—Captain Peter Bernard and Charles Thompson—were knowledgeable travelers and the circumstances of their deaths is unknown (see Stefansson 1922:646–659). Kuptana was quite young at the time of these events and he may be combining the two incidents.

55

When we came in sight of it, a crowd of about a hundred men, women, and children came out to meet us, practically the entire population. Among them, I recognized several acquaintances from my short visit to these people the spring of 1911, but several I remembered I did not see. Inquiries brought about the fact that two of those with whom I had particularly associated had died, but that most who were not now here in Minto Inlet were supposed to be in Prince Albert Sound. It seems that about a year ago the group of about two hundred and twenty people found by me in the Sound in 1911 had divided into two nearly equal sections, one remaining in the Sound and the other coming north into Minto Inlet and amalgamating with the twenty or thirty people whom in my previous books I have spoken of as a separate people. I now learned that from their own point of view they were always the same people and that any one bears the name of Minto Inlet or Prince Albert Sound (Kanghiryuakjagmiut and Kanghiryuarmiut respectively) according to which of these districts he inhabits any particular year (Stefansson 1921:418).

Thus, Stefansson discovered that the Copper Inuit of Minto Inlet and Prince Albert Sound did not constitute two distinct groups, but that population movement between the two locations, and across to Banks Island, was a common feature of their nomadic way of life.

The Inuit village consisted of a long row of snowhouses built under a steep bank. This was the only location where suitable snow could be found for making snowhouses. Since the ice on Minto Inlet had not yet frozen over, the people were waiting for the winter to advance sufficiently so that they could move their settlement onto the ice and commence breathing-hole sealing. Such autumn settlements along the coast were fairly typical among the Copper Inuit, as people gradually gathered after the summer season of wandering in the interior. At this place there would be much socializing and preparing of clothes and tools for the upcoming winter.

Banks Island

Albert Palvik. We used to travel over to Banks Island and winter at DeSalis Bay. People before me always used to travel to Banks Island, mostly to hunt polar bear or musk ox. I spent four or five winters there in one stretch without coming back to Victoria Island. I stayed at a place a little north of DeSalis Bay called Naksavik [Naksaviq] hunting caribou. It was a good place for musk ox hunting. There are lots of horns over there too. There were also lots of seals at DeSalis Bay. We lived not only on caribou but on seals too. We also did some trapping while we were over there. During the summers, there were lots of signs of foxes, but they seemed to have moved away when it was time to trap. We got some foxes, but not lots.

Stefansson noted that some snowhouses were made with a single dome, some with two, and others with three. The largest house in the village, that of an elder named Hitkoak, measured thirty feet across and was almost eleven feet high and held two large bed platforms. When an impromptu reception was held for Stefansson, Hitkoak's snowhouse accommodated seventy-five people. Stefansson reported that there was ample food. Some of the people had just finished fishing and hunting caribou at lakes to the northeast. A number of seals and polar bears had been killed and a party from Banks Island had brought sledges loaded with dried goosemeat from molting geese that had been killed north of Cape Kellet, on the southwest coast of Banks Island (Stefansson 1921:420). When Stefansson took leave of this group of Inuit, he tried to convince several families to spend the winter near his base camp at Deans Dundas Bay. All refused, insisting that seals could not be found in that part of the strait (Prince of Wales Strait).

Stefansson's books are useful not only because they include details of Copper Inuit culture but because they provide the names of individuals with whom he came into contact (and whose descendants can be traced through genealogical interviews). One such individual was a man from Minto Inlet named Kullak (Kudlak), whom Stefansson met on Banks Island in August 1915. Kullak, accompanied by his wife, Neriyok (Nigiyok), his six-year-old son Herona, and his young daughter Titalik (most likely Susie Tiktalik), had spent the spring camped on the ice in Prince Wales Strait and had later moved to Banks Island in order to hunt musk ox and geese. When Stefansson was preparing to leave Kullak's camp, Kullak gave him a pair of white sealskin slippers. Stefansson recalled: "When I asked him the reason he said that his wife expected the birth of a baby in a few days and he wanted me to see to it that she would have an easy delivery and that the child should be a boy. . . . Kullak had not the slightest doubt that I could by magical means control the birth both as to its safety and the sex of the child" (Stefansson 1921:371). Stefansson's acceptance of the gift was to have dire consequences. The following year, Kullak accused Stefansson of murder because his wife had died several weeks after the birth. Kullak demanded restitution from Stefansson; otherwise, he said, he would be forced to kill Stefansson, or a member of his expedition. The conflict was resolved when Kullak was given a rifle and a considerable amount of ammunition, both items that were then relatively rare possessions among the northern Copper Inuit (Stefansson 1921:566–567).

In addition to collecting detailed ethnographic information on the Copper Inuit, both the northern and southern parties of the Canadian Arctic Expedition took many photographs of Copper Inuit life, supplementing the smaller collection of photographs taken by Stefansson during his 1908–1912 expedition. One of the members of the northern party was George H. Wilkins, the expedition's professional photographer from 1913 to 1916. Wilkins produced both still photographs and movies of the Prince Albert Sound people. This motion-picture film footage is the earliest moving film footage taken anywhere in the Canadian Arctic. Although the film footage was never edited into a documentary film, it is currently stored in the Public Archives of Canada in Ottawa.

The southern party, based at Bernard Harbor, had the expedition's official anthropologist, Diamond Jenness. Although Stefansson's writings provide much useful information concerning traditional Copper Inuit society, Jenness made a more systematic study of the Copper Inuit. Working south of Prince Albert Sound, Jenness concentrated on the groups living around Coronation Gulf and Dolphin and Union Strait.

After learning the Copper Inuit dialect, Jenness left the mainland and spent the better part of the spring, summer, and fall of 1915 traveling on the southern part of Victoria Island with a family that had adopted him. Jenness wanted to cut himself off completely from his fellow expedition members and they remained behind in the base camp at Bernard Harbor. As a lone white man living with the Inuit, Jenness (or Jennessi as he was called by the Inuit) hoped to live among the people and observe the details of Inuit summer life in a way that no white person had so far been able to do. Jenness later wrote:

> It was for this purpose, indeed, that I had cut myself adrift from the rest of the expedition until the winter when the strait would freeze over again and allow me to return to Bernard Harbor. In the back of my mind lay also another plan. Sixty miles to the

northward was Prince Albert Sound, the home of an Eskimo tribe
that I had not yet visited. Each summer, a few of the Sound
people met and traded with the Eskimos from Dolphin and Union
Strait somewhere in the interior of Wollaston Land, and Ikpuck
[Jenness's adopted father] who was born in this region, promised
to guide our party to their usual place of rendezvous (Jenness
1928:109).

Jenness and his adopted family eventually made camp along-
side Lake Tahiryuak (Quunnguq), just south of Prince Albert
Sound, and met two Kangiryuarmiut families. These people
reported that most of their group had gone north of the sound
to fish and hunt caribou near another lake, also called Lake
Tahiryuak. The visitors also reported that copper deposits could
be found in a cliff near the northern lake. The two days of the
Prince Albert Sound people's visit were filled with gossip, trade,
and dances. Jenness reports that these visitors watched him
with great interest because "only one white man had crossed
their lives before and had vanished before they knew him inti-
mately" (Jenness 1928:123). The white man referred to was
most likely Stefansson, who had visited the Prince Albert Sound
people in 1911. Jenness, in a diary published by his son in 1991,
recorded his meeting with the Kangiryuarmiut as follows:

> Tuesday, June 1st: A cold day, cloudy, with a light west wind. A
> family of *Kanghirjuarmiut* appeared about noon, with a sled, a
> man Kunana, his wife Nateksina, their adopted baby Allikumik,
> and a young man Imeraq. All have dark black hair, with a brown
> tinge towards the light, but the man has a tawny moustache and
> beard, both rather sparse. . . . As soon as they set up their tent
> and we all had partaken of their food inside it, two of the men
> set to work to make a dance house of snow-blocks and roofed it
> with skins and my sled cover. Then came the dance of welcome,
> interrupted about midnight by the arrival of a second sled with
> three more *Kanghirjuarmiut* natives [Nilgak, his wife Otoayoak,
> and their eleven-year-old son, Akkoakhion]. Again we partook of
> their food, but it was too late to resume the dance, so one by one
> we turned in at 3 a.m. (1991:447).

Traveling to Lake Tahiryuak (Quunnguq)

Albert Palvik. I was raised in Prince Albert Sound and remember
these two men, Kunana and Nilgak, from when I was a young
boy. Kunana was Mark Emerak's father. He had another son who

Fig. 2.9. Two Kangiryuarmiut men, Kunana and Nilgak, eating boiled caribou
meat at Quunnguq Lake (also referred to
as Lake Tahiryuak), south of Prince Albert
Sound. The photograph was taken by anthropologist Diamond Jenness when he
was traveling in southern Victoria Island
with a Puivlingmiut (Puivlirmiut) family
during the summer and fall of 1915. At
that time, Quunnguq was a traditional
gathering place for the Puivlingmiut
(from southern Victoria Island) and the
Kangiryuarmiut (from Prince Albert
Sound). The groups would meet to trade
and socialize. Quunnguq was also a favorite spring fishing site for both groups due
to the appearance of a large crack (*quunnguq*) on the lake in springtime. The crack
accounts for the lake's name. Photo taken
in June 1915 by Diamond Jenness. Courtesy of the Canadian Museum of Civilization, No. 36967.

was about the same age as myself. We used to play together, *Early* but he died at an early age. Nilgak's son was Akkowakiut who *Contact* was Harry Egotak's father. Akkowakiut married Pappidluk, who *History* later married Harry Niakoaluk.

In those days, people traveled all over Prince Albert Sound and in winter would come down around the islands where there was good seal hunting. In the summer, people from Prince Albert Sound would travel down to Tahiryuak [Quunnguq] where they would meet the people from the mainland and the southern part of Victoria Island. They got together to trade, socialize, and hold dances. In those days, it was hard to get driftwood in Prince Albert Sound. But there was lots of driftwood in the south, so we would trade copper knives and other things made from copper for wood which we would use to make sleds. This kind of trade went on long before the white man came up here.

Agnes Nigiyok. That Kunana is Emerak's father. Old man. He wasn't able to move or do things for himself then. That's when they left him on the land in an area where the land level was higher. Emeraks [Emerak and his wife Otoayok] had left him alone. Otoayok used to say this to us. We used to feel sorry for and compassion for that Kunana fellow being left out on the land. It was towards the fall time when people started to get together. Emeraks said that they had left him right on a dry area so that he died of thirst. He must have been thirsting quite a bit. His insides must have been really dry. He would search for water. He wasn't able to walk and that's why they left him.

Frank Kuptana. This was when a lot of people used to get together to do their fishing, and they would also have dances when they got together there. Here at Lake Tahiryuak. They would fish and dance. That Lake Tahiryuak has a quunnguq. A lake with a quunnguq has a crack in the ice where people would fish. They would get to the lake when it started warming up. People from Prince Albert Sound and the Read Island area would walk to the lake, meet there, and fish and dance with the qilaut [drum].

Kunana and Nilgak at Quunnguq

Albert Palvik: I remember seeing those two men when I was a young boy. Kunana was the father of Mark Imerak, and Nilgak was the father of Akkowakiuk [Harry Egotak's father]. People from Prince Albert Sound used to travel to this lake where they

61

would meet the people from the mainland and the southern part
of Victoria Island. They got together to trade, socialize, and hold
dances. In those days, it was hard to get driftwood in Prince
Albert Sound. But there was lots of driftwood in the south and
we would trade copper knives and other things made of copper
for wood which we would use to make sleds.

Jenness did not make it to Prince Albert Sound, but he had
satisfied his curiosity that the Prince Albert Sound people were,
as to language and culture, very similar to the Copper Inuit of
Dolphin and Union Strait. Toward the end of the summer,
Jenness and his adopted family made the slow migration back
to the southern coast, fishing and hunting caribou along the
way. At that time of year, food shortages were common and
the Inuit would go for days without sighting caribou or catching
fish. Jenness was impressed by the endurance and patience of
his traveling companions: "The experience [of starvation] was
no novelty in their lives; they merely tightened their belts,
trudged steadily forward a dozen or fifteen miles, and said
smilingly, 'If we sight no caribou today we will tomorrow; or,
if not tomorrow, certainly the day after'" (Jenness 1928:219).

After his extended research visit to the land of the Copper Inuit,
Jenness wrote two definitive books about the people with whom
he lived and traveled: *The Life of the Copper Eskimos* (1922) and
The People of the Twilight (1928).[7] Stefansson, working to the
north, and Jenness, to the south, documented well the traditional
culture of the Copper Inuit. This scholarship was completed just
in time, for the isolation of the Copper Inuit was soon shattered
permanently by the activities of traders, missionaries, and other
representatives of southern culture. As Jenness wrote years later
in his epilogue to *The People of the Twilight*:

> Even as we sailed away traders entered their country seeking
> fox-furs; and for those pelts so useless for real clothing they
> offered rifles, shot-guns, steel tools, and other goods that prom-
> ised to make life easier. So the Eskimos abandoned their commu-
> nal seal hunts and scattered in isolated families along the coasts
> in order to trap white foxes during the winter when the fur of

7. The diaries of Diamond Jenness have recently been edited by his son,
Stuart Jenness, and published by the Canadian Museum of Civilization (see
Jenness 1991). This diary gives a detailed daily account of the anthropologist's
work and travels with the Copper Inuit.

Fig. 2.10. Repairing cooking pot. Oqalluk, a Copper Inuit man, is seen repairing a cooking pot, made from a kerosene can, while a companion, Tuhajok, makes arrow heads from a caribou antler, southwestern Victoria Island, June 23, 1915. Source of caption: Jenness 1991:467. Photo by Diamond Jenness. Courtesy of the Canadian Museum of Civilization, No. 37052.

that animal reaches its prime. Their dispersal loosened the old communal ties that had held the families together. The men no longer labored for the entire group, but hunted and trapped each one for his family alone. . . . The commercial world of the white man had caught the Eskimos in its mesh, destroying their self-sufficiency and independence, and made them economically its slaves. Only in one respect did it benefit them: it lessened the danger of those unpredictable famines which had overtaken them every ten or fifteen years, bringing suffering and death to young and old without distinction (Jenness 1928:240).

Traveling

Rene Taipana. When I first remember. My first memories—like when I first woke up myself.* People in the spring would gather at the coast. It was in the spring—like this time of year. We would travel to a lake and stay there until late spring waiting for the land to dry up so we could hunt caribou. We would fish and

*During interviews, many Inuit elders used the expression "when I first woke up" to refer to their earliest memories.

63

get an occasional caribou for meat, while waiting for the hair of the caribou to become good for clothing. That's how people lived back then. And when the land was good to travel on and when the caribou hair and skin were good, we traveled inland hunting for caribou—for clothing and food. We fished along the way, going to where there are kiidjiyuq [fish that sit in warm water] in mouths of rivers and along the shores of lakes. We lived inland until it started to get dark out. We used to live on the land that way throughout the summer. And when it was around the end of August or September, we would start our gradual trip back to the coast. When the caribou hair is thick, we would hunt for those caribou with the thick hair for the outer parka called qullitaq. That's when the weather is starting to get cold. That's when we started our walk back to the ocean.

At that time, the beginning of our trip back to the coast was called hivuqamuyuq. When the lakes started to freeze over, then we would know it was around the fall season. We made sleds with our caribou skins which were called uniutik [skins dragged on the ground] rather than alliak. And then it's late fall. That's when the ocean starts to freeze over and we leave our trip from hunting caribou with the thick hair and descend to the coast. That trip was called ataupluta. That was our way of life.

When we got to the coast, we built our igloos. We finished building our igloos at a place where we left our spring caches of seal fat from seals caught the previous winter. These caches were for this specific time of year when we head back for the coastline. That's where we camped while we sewed clothing to use when the sun starts to shine again after Christmas. That clothing was to be worn then.

Sam Oliktoak. In the fall, when the ocean first freezes up along the coastline, we built snowhouses and made our clothing. At the end of Christmas, when we have done our clothing, we headed out on the ice. Before we left for the ice, we spent a day playing games and feasting. Food of all kinds was gathered and prepared. That's how we feasted then.

Rene Taipana. Nattiqut. That's what we called the platform on which the food was placed on top of a sealskin. We feasted in a snowhouse built for that purpose every year.

Sam Oliktoak. We built three snowhouses. In the middle to connect the three, we built a large snowhouse. This is where the dancing took place and the playing of games—in the center of the igloo. Some akhunaaq [thongs made from sealskin] were put up for people to swing on.

Rene Taipana. My parents would talk about those times. Those are the times that I remember. They danced with a qilaut, an Eskimo drum.

Sam Oliktoak. They would gather there to play games and dance for one day. They danced until late at night, and after that day, we were all ready to travel down onto the ocean. We had to wait for the sea-ice to be covered with hard packed snow so we could build snowhouses out on the ice. We also had to wait until the snow on the ice was good for drinking water.

Rene Taipana. That's right. We had to wait until our snow wasn't salty tasting for snow water. Even without any doctors, people knew back then that the snow on the sea-ice is salty with the first snowfall. So they didn't go out on the ice right away.

3. Interlude

Traditional Copper Inuit Culture, 1850 to 1910

THE ETHNOGRAPHIC WORKS of Diamond Jenness and Vilhjalmur Stefansson combined with the recollections of Inuit elders provide an intimate and detailed account of Copper Inuit culture prior to the arrival of fur traders, missionaries, police, and government administrators.[1] In language and culture, the various groups identified by anthropologists as Copper Inuit display a distinctiveness that separates them from the Mackenzie Delta people to the west and the Netsilik people to the east.

Prior to the concentration of the population into settlements and towns, the Copper Inuit were composed of a number of fairly distinct regional subgroups. The names of these subgroups ended with the suffix -miut which (as mentioned in the preface) translates as "people of." Stefansson identified nineteen of these groups; Jenness documented seventeen (see Damas 1984:401). Examples include the Kangiryuarmiut of Prince Albert Sound ("people of the big sound"), the Nagyuktogmiut of southwestern Victoria Island ("people of the caribou antler"),

---

1. To the list of valuable records should be added the works of the Greenlandic ethnographer Knud Ramussen, especially his *Intellectual Culture of the Copper Eskimos* (1932). Since Rasmussen worked primarily in the eastern Copper Inuit region, he is not mentioned in the main part of our text. Nevertheless, Rasmussen's contributions to the study of the Copper, Netsilik, and Iglulik peoples are seminal works in the field of Inuit ethnography.

66

Fig. 3.1. *Travelling Couple*, Holman Print Collection, 1984. Lithograph by Peter Aliknak (artist) and Peter Palvik (printer). Edition: 50. Courtesy of the Holman Eskimo Cooperative.

Fig. 3.2. Group of Kangiryuarmiut children in front of snowhouses, Prince Albert Sound, 1911. This photograph was taken by Vilhjalmur Stefansson during his first meeting with the people of Prince Albert Sound. Courtesy of the Dartmouth College Library, Stefansson Collection.

and the Umingmaktomiut of Bathurst Inlet ("people of the musk oxen"). When added on to a particular geographic location, the *miut* suffix simply referred to all those people who exploited that particular hunting area. Membership in these groups was quite fluid. Individuals could easily move from one summer hunting territory to another.

Despite uniformity of culture and language, the various *miut* displayed minor differences, based upon their adaptation to local resources. While some groups were primarily dependent on seal and polar bear, others focused on caribou and musk oxen. Although people exploited whatever resources happened to be available in their particular region, the pattern of subsistence and social organization was fundamentally the same. At the time of contact, the total population of Copper Inuit was probably no more than eight hundred to nine hundred, scattered over a vast territory of arctic tundra, probably exceeding 80,000 square miles.

Environment

The environment of the Copper Inuit is mostly treeless arctic tundra, although some wooded areas can be found in the southernmost reaches of Copper Inuit territory. The climate is severe, with winter temperatures frequently reaching −50 F. (−45C.) in some areas. The monthly mean of the coldest month of the year, February, is between −20 and −28F. (−29C. and −33C.), and the monthly mean of the warmest month, July, is in the high 40s (7 to 10C.). Precipitation is minimal. Most of this falls as snow and accumulates in high drifts as a result of blowing winds. The amount of sunlight varies dramatically by season. In the Holman region, for example, the sun drops below the horizon in the third week in November and stays down until January 16 or 17. During these two months, there is only a brief daily period of twilight at midday which becomes progressively darker and shorter until the winter solstice. In summer, the sun stays above the horizon for an equivalent period, providing, as it circles, long hours of sunlight for people to hunt, fish and travel.

As is true of much of the Canadian Arctic, the tundra ecosystem is characterized by extremely low biological productivity. Significantly less energy is absorbed by the arctic ecosystem, compared with more temperate regions. Almost no energy is absorbed in winter. Even in summer, with the sun above the horizon twenty four hours a day, the sun's rays are extremely weak, contributing little radiant energy to either the tundra or the marine ecosystem. The net result is that the Arctic operates under a significant energy deficit, with great implications for plants and animals and for the people who depend upon them for survival.

In winter, the straits, sounds, and gulfs in Copper Inuit territory are frozen in a continuous sheet of ice from October or November until July. This is ideal habitat for ringed seals, which prefer solid, landfast ice with early formation in fall and late breakup in summer.

Seasonal Round

Since the environment was marked (as it still is) by dramatic seasonal fluctuations in temperature, light duration, snowfall, ice conditions, and game availability, Copper Inuit families had to display great flexibility in economic and social organization in order to adapt successfully to the demands of each season. One of the most important phases of Copper Inuit life was the winter season of breathing-hole sealing. This was the coldest

Fig. 3.3. Copper Inuit snowhouse on ocean ice, Duke of York Archipelago, 1915. The wide entrances of these snowhouses provided protection against the wind as well as storage space for food and equipment. Note that the sled has been raised up on snowblocks to prevent it from being drifted over with snow. Photo by Diamond Jenness. Courtesy of the Canadian Museum of Civilization, No. 37018.

and darkest time of year and it tested the Inuit's ability to survive such harsh conditions. Large snowhouse communities typically formed out on the sea-ice in locations close to good sealing grounds. Movement onto the ice was accomplished as soon as ice conditions became stable enough for travel and camping, ideally by late November or early December. These snowhouse villages varied in size from about 50 individuals to as many as 150. Damas (1984:400) estimates that the mean size ranged from about 91 to 117. Most of the people who resided in these snowhouse villages were related, either closely or distantly, but many nonrelatives were included as well. Villages moved when sealing became unproductive, with smaller groups occasionally splitting off.

Camping in Winter

Ruth Nigiyonak. I remember camping in the winter season out on the frozen sea ice. As a child, during the winter, the people never stayed on the land. When winter came, the people moved out on the ice. For the winter, the people would build a large snowhouse with a big workspace in the center. From the sides, they would build tunnels. And at the end of each tunnel, a family would build their living quarters. The center was a work space or a place to gather for games, drum dances, and stories. That was repeated each year.

During the winter, an elaborate system of seal sharing (*piqati-giit*) among both kin and nonkin was the dominant form of food distribution. Breathing-hole sealing required a degree of cooperation among hunters, who dispersed over a wide area to cover as many breathing holes as possible. Since each seal maintains a number of breathing holes, this strategy maximized the chances that at least one hunter from a group would be successful. Once caught, the seal was divided into twelve to fourteen parts, each part given to a predetermined exchange partner who would reciprocate sometime in the future with the same body part. Names were applied to seal-sharing partners based on the animal part exchanged: flipper companion, liver companion, and so forth. A man's seal-sharing partners were usually assigned by parents and other adults at the time of a hunter's first kill. Kinship factors were irrelevant to such partnerships since both kin and nonkin could be included in these networks.

Winter subsistence pursuits also included polar bear hunting in some areas, the importance of which for subsistence varied from year to year depending upon availability. The Copper Inuit who wintered between Banks Island and northwestern Victoria Island relied more heavily upon polar bear than other Copper Inuit groups.

Winter was an important time for community social festivities, which were conducted in a large, ceremonial snowhouse, or *qagli*. Because cold, darkness, and the frequent blizzards limited the amount of time that men could stay out hunting, people would pass their time playing games, drum dancing, and occasionally observing shamanic performances. Given the size of some snowhouse communities, it was not unusual for the *qagli* to be bursting with observers and participants. The Copper Inuit spent much of the spring, summer, and early fall wandering on the tundra in small family groups, and winter truly represented the climax of community social life.

With the arrival of warmer weather and longer daylight hours in April and May, the Copper Inuit started hunting for basking seals. This was a more individualistic pursuit, requiring the hunter to walk and crawl great distances to harpoon seals basking next to a crack or seal hole. Breathing-hole sealing, as well, continued into May, and some Copper Inuit made excursions to hunt polar bears as their period of hibernation ended. By

Fig. 3.4. Copper Inuit traveling by sled over the ice. Before the introduction of trapping, a Copper Inuit family rarely owned more than two or three dogs, if that. Sleds were often dragged by humans. Photo by Diamond Jenness. Courtesy of the Canadian Museum of Civilization, No. 20288.

spring, the large snowhouse communities usually started to break into smaller groups, each headed in a different direction. Movement was initially along the coastline, because the tundra would still be wet and unpleasant for travel. Eventually, the ocean ice was abandoned altogether, marking the beginning of the inland phase of the yearly cycle.

The abandonment of snowhouses in spring is understandable. As warmer weather conditions made the interiors wet and uncomfortable, modified snowhouses were made. These consisted of the lower half of a snowhouse with a skin roof over it. As the year progressed, skin tents replaced these modified snowhouses as people moved up to the land.

Eider Duck Hunt

William Kuptana. The first duck I got was from a small pond. It was shared by the elders as tradition called for. It is a custom to share your first kill with your elders. When the ducks come up in the spring, because of the lack of open water along the

Fig. 3.5. Copper Inuit family Traveling over the tundra. The photographer identifies these people as Higilak and Ikpukkuaq near Lake Anmaloqtoq, southwestern Victoria Island, June 1915. With the melting of the snow, sleds were abandoned and possessions were carried in backpacks. Note the fishing leister being carried by the women. Photo by Diamond Jenness. Courtesy of the Canadian Museum of Civilization, No. 36989.

shore, they are found mostly on the mainland. This is where I got my first eider duck. Later, I was with a group of hunters. We came upon a large flock of eiders. They had alighted on the shore lead and were resting and feeding. As we approached, some flew away, while others dove into the water. We immediately advanced as swiftly as possible before the ducks emerged from the water. I waited for the ducks to come up for air. As they came up, I was lucky enough to get one by using a bow and arrow. That was my second duck. It was so difficult to hunt ducks with bows and arrows in those days that if a person got at least three ducks, it was considered a large catch.

Traditional Copper Inuit Culture

Once spring arrived, Copper Inuit families spread out over a large area of the tundra, seeking fish and waterfowl. Although caribou were also beginning to return in both small and large herds, they were infrequently hunted in early summer due to leanness and the poor quality of their skins. Before the introduction of firearms, the number of ducks and geese harvested was probably quite small. Most food in the early summer came from fishing. In certain areas, such as Victoria Island, most fishing was done on inland lakes, where it was especially productive as the ice began to melt along the lakeshore. In other areas, mostly on the mainland, Copper Inuit had access to early summer runs of char which were intercepted at stone weirs built in streams and rivers. The Copper Inuit prepared dried lake-trout and char for use throughout summer and fall.

Summer Fishing

William Kuptana. During the summer, the Copper Inuit would pile up stone corrals in the shallow streams to trap the fish. When the fish swam through to the corrals, the Inuit would block the entrance to prevent the fish from escaping. The take from the corral would total a few hundred fish. The various ways they'd prepare the fish is by drying and then smoking to preserve it over the winter months. The remainder of the catch was then buried with stone caches that were built so other predators could not help themselves to the fish.

Double Tents

Frank Kuptana. Those double tents were called "paaqtiriat." People would put the poles together like this and put skins over so

73

Fig. 3.6. Double tent of two Kangiryuarmiut families at Lake Tahiry-uak (Lake Quunnguq), south of Prince Albert Sound, June 1915. Photo by Diamond Jenness. Courtesy of the Canadian Museum of Civilization, No. 36985.

that if they had a big family, they could camp together, or for parents and their in-laws. I remember seeing these kinds of caribou tents when I was younger. Even friends would camp like this.

Spring was also the time of year when Copper Inuit families traveled great distances for the purposes of trade or for obtaining valued raw materials, such as wood and soapstone. Trade was initiated with other Copper Inuit groups, as well as more distant peoples. The Copper Inuit were remarkable travelers. Stefansson described trading expeditions in which Prince Albert Sound people traveled as far as the Thelon River on the west coast of Hudson Bay in order to trade with the Caribou Inuit. Since the Copper Inuit did not have many dogs, these trading expeditions might last several months, or even years, as families slowly progressed over the tundra, hunting and fishing along the way. Their journeys occurred in stages, starting out with sleds and then switching to backpacking as the snow disappeared. Whether trading was with other Copper Inuit or with other groups, special trading partnerships were often established to guarantee peaceful relations.

Caribou Hunting

William Kuptana. I remember being packed going inland in the summer. When we were out of food, we'd eat seal fat out of the pouch. My parents would also carry a sealskin bag filled with seal blood. We'd drink out of that when we were thirsty.

While we were treking inland, food would become scarce. My parents killed a lemming and cooked it. I didn't want to eat it, but they talked to me so I had to eat it. I didn't want to be left behind. We'd keep walking and looking for caribou. When we'd come to a lake that was still frozen over, they would make an agluaq (fishing hole). Hook and spear were used to catch fish. By fishing, that would prevent us from starving. Also, when the ice is gone in the river, they would fish by using spears and wading in after them.

After that, we would go wandering off into the land looking for caribou. We had no guns. Finally, when we found a small herd, the men would then build a small projection of stone slabs on a high point of land to act as a rouse to startle the fleeing caribou. The women would advance toward the caribou, humming as they approached the herd. As the caribou approached the lair where the men were hiding, the men would then kill the closest ones, the ones that they could reach.

The kill meant, "Feast." The family would eat everything: stomach, entrails, marrow. For instance, the entrails would be cleaned out and then cooked. After they were cooked, the entrails would be eaten with seal oil. The extra meat would be cut up to make dried meat.

The primary economic and cooperative unit in summer and early fall was the nuclear family. A family might be joined by other families, either related or unrelated, at times, most notably in productive fishing or caribou areas. At other times, families would wander on their own. There was no hard and fast rule regarding the composition of summer groups. Individual families made their own decisions about whom to travel with and for how long. In short, summer was the season of greatest dispersal for the Copper Inuit, largely due to the scattered nature of food resources. The warm summer months were not a time of plenty for the Copper Inuit. As Diamond Jenness (1922:123–24) noted: "The traveller will find scattered families roaming about from place to place, here today and gone tomorrow in their restless search for game. Days of feasting alternate with days of fasting according to their failure or success. No fowl of the air, no creature of the land, no fish of the waters is too great or too small to attract their notice at this time."

The scarcity of food in spring and summer was partially alleviated in the late summer/early fall (August and September) when caribou hunting accelerated. At this time of year the caribou are fattest and their hides are ideal for making clothes. Usually a number of families would cooperate in the hunting of caribou using caribou drives set up on the tundra. These drives usually consisted of rows of stone piles set in two converging lines. Women and children chased the caribou into the mouth of the drive. At the narrow end of the drive, men hid themselves and prepared to dispatch the caribou with lances and arrows. Another technique, more commonly used on the mainland, involved hunting caribou from kayaks at crossing places in lakes. If a caribou drive was successful, much of the meat would be dried and stored for use during the lean autumn months.

First Hunt

William Kuptana. When I first killed a caribou, my biological father started wrestling with me as it is a custom to try to put a young hunter on top of the caribou corpse. After that, the hunting party told me to get the ulimuan [a chisel-like instrument with a blade at a forty-five degree angle from the handle]. So I got one out of the pack-sack to open its head as it is a custom that a young man do that for a first kill. After I had chopped its skull, the elders started eating its inner membrane, or as it is usually called, the brain. Then, after the feast, the hunting party resumed their search for the tuktuvialuit (Banks Island caribou). From spring to autumn, the hunting party would kill, store, and go on searching until it was too cold to hunt. Finally, returning to their wintering grounds, they'd wait for winter huddled in their sealskin tents for a time.

Early fall, however, was a productive time for spear fishing in rivers and streams. This was the time of year in many river systems when arctic char returned to lakes after spending much of the summer feeding in the ocean. The char were fattest at

Fig. 3.7. Copper Inuit fishing at stone weir, Nulahugyuk Creek, near Bernard Harbour, June 1916. Photo by Diamond Jenness. Courtesy of the Canadian Museum of Civilization, No. 37078.

this time of year and hence a desirable food item. Families arrived at fishing sites early enough to repair the stone weirs, which might have been disturbed the previous winter by ice movement. The repair work completed, families waited for the run to start. In areas with large char runs, a number of families might congregate. A successful fishing season was marked by great numbers of filleted fish hung to dry. Much of this fish, as well as the caribou, was stored for use during late fall and early winter.

Autumn

William Kuptana. When fall approached, they [Inuit] treked back to their wintering grounds. Along the way when they killed caribou, they built stone caches to store the food for winter. The cache also served as protection from scavengers such as wolves and foxes. Sometimes, too, depending on the weather, the caribou meat was cut up to make more dried meat. The dried meat was lighter to carry and fermentation didn't take place as quickly as it did with raw meat if not eaten right away.

When they arrived in the vicinity of their wintering grounds, they started fishing through the frozen ice on the lakes. Arctic char was baited by a polar bear tooth, then speared. The fish was then scooped with a sealskin bag wrapped to a wooden or bone handle by a sealskin thong. They filled those bags with fish. The preferred catch was male fish and the preferred area of fishing was in the spawning areas.

Fishing for char was done through October when the ice got too thick to chop through.

As the fall season brought colder and windier weather, groups generally met at traditional fall gathering places where women prepared the winter's clothing. Once families moved out onto the ice, women were forbidden to sew, and all had to be accomplished at the gathering place. While women prepared the clothing, men made ready the winter hunting equipment. Hunting and fishing continued, but on a limited scale. At this time of year, game was relatively scarce. Often, families had to live on accumulated food reserves. Once ice conditions permitted the migration on to the ice, the winter season of sealing and polar bear hunting would commence.

Social Organization

Compared with other Inuit groups in Canada and Alaska, the Copper Inuit had a relatively simple form of social organization.

Fig. 3.8. Copper Inuit in Coronation Gulf area giving peace signal. The photographer, Diamond Jenness, said the Copper Inuit of this region would raise their hands over their heads when being approached to show that they were friendly and carried no weapons (see chapter 2 for description of other signs). Courtesy of the Canadian Museum Civilization, No. 37105.

Since there were no permanent villages or camps other than the midwinter snowhouse communities, there was essentially no form of political organization beyond the nuclear family. Whereas the Inuit of the eastern Arctic were organized into large extended families (*ilagiit*), united under a headman, or *isumataq*, the Copper Inuit did not have such large extended families, nor such formalized leadership roles. Kin relationships were recognized with first and second cousins, as well as with more distant relatives, but these relationships did not play as significant a role in food sharing, residential organization, or cooperative hunting as they did in other areas of the Arctic. Thus while food-sharing and cooperative hunting were usually restricted to the extended family unit in the eastern Arctic, for the Copper Inuit such activity frequently involved nonrelatives. This was especially true with regard to the system of seal-sharing partnerships, which as mentioned earlier could be made up of non-kin as well as kin. In this respect, the Copper Inuit were—and still are—unique among most Canadian Inuit groups (with the possible exception of the Caribou Inuit of the Keewatin) in their form of social organization.

Material Culture

Like most Canadian Inuit, the Copper Inuit had a very sophisticated and highly specialized technology for exploiting the resources of the arctic ecosystem. The material hallmark, of course, was the use of copper, which was exploited to manufacture tools such as ulus, knives, and harpoon heads. The copper was surface-mined at several locations, primarily in the valley of the Coppermine River, then cold-hammered into usable shapes. The Copper Inuit were also well known for their soapstone lamps. The quality of the soapstone in Copper Inuit territory, specifically the Tree River area, was vastly superior to that in other regions. There is evidence of an active trade in Copper Inuit soapstone around the mid-1800s. One researcher has suggested that the Kangiryuarmiut of the Holman region acted as middlemen in trading Coronation Gulf soapstone lamps for Russian iron, from Siberia (see Morrison 1991). The soapstone may have traveled as far as Kotzebue Sound in western Alaska and perhaps even across the Bering Strait.

The dome-shaped snowhouse was the dominant winter residence for all Copper Inuit groups, being made of large snow-blocks placed in an inward-leaning spiral. As noted by both

Stefansson and Jenness, these snowhouses could be arranged
in a multitude of floor plans. For example, two adjacent snowhouses could be joined together with a short passage; or they
could share the same entrance. In December 1915, Jenness observed a large ceremonial snowhouse with four smaller exten-
sions connected to it. The flexibility of snow as a building material clearly allowed numerous permutations of basic snowhouse
design, reflecting both kin relations and friendships between
families.

The basic plan of the Copper Inuit snowhouse followed that
of other Canadian Inuit groups. The entrance passage sloped
downward until the main chamber was reached. The slope
provided a "cold trap" that prevented cold air from blowing in
to the living area. Inside the main chamber was a sleeping
platform (made of snow), elevated several feet off the floor.
There the family both slept and carried out other activities. A
soapstone lamp (*qudlik*) was positioned to one side of the sleeping platform, or, in some cases, suspended from the ceiling by
a skin rope. The qudlik was used for cooking and also provided
heat and light.

Travel in winter was by sled, pulled by people and dogs. In
comparison with other Canadian Inuit, the Copper Inuit had
few dogs. Jenness noted that a well-to-do family might have
as many as two or three, but rarely more. Researchers have
explained the small number of dogs as being the result of the
Copper Inuit residing in one of the harsher and less productive
regions of the central Arctic. Given the scarcity of animal life
and the fact that the Copper Inuit did not hunt large marine
mammals, such as walrus and whales, they were unable to feed
large numbers of dogs, as could be done in the Igloolik area or
on Baffin Island. Midwinter travel required men, women, and
older children to pull the sled (*qamutik*), with the help of a
small number of dogs. In summer, the sled was cached near
the coast and all belongings were backpacked overland. Dogs
also helped carry the load in dog packs.

The Copper Inuit also made and used kayaks. These were not
the elaborate, oceangoing kayaks of eastern Arctic Inuit, but
relatively short, wide kayaks made for use mostly on lakes when
caribou hunting. Marine-mammal hunting by kayak was not
developed in the Copper Inuit region as it was in many other
areas of the Arctic.

Primary hunting weapons included the toggle headed harpoon (for seal hunting), the bola (for bird hunting), the fish
leister (for fishing), the spear (for bear hunting), and the com-

pound bow and arrows (for musk ox and caribou hunting). The seal harpoon was undoubtedly the most important of these and was part of a larger inventory of breathing-hole sealing equipment that included snow probes, icepicks, and seal indicators.

The sophistication of Copper Inuit hunting equipment was matched only by the efficiency and technological sophistication of Inuit skin-clothing. Each item was custom-tailored. Copper Inuit women were expert seamstresses, producing caribou skin and sealskin parkas, pants, boots, and mitts. Most impressive were boots, with soles made from the skin of the bearded seal (*ugyuk*), sewn so as to be completely watertight. A man's ability to hunt was clearly related to his wife's ability to sew warm, dry, comfortable clothing.

Marriage

It was considered highly desirable by all Copper Inuit to marry and bear offspring. The man or woman who failed to marry

Fig. 3.9. Two Copper Inuit with hunting bows. The bows were generally made from caribou antler or musk ox horn bound together with sinew. Photo by G. H. Wilkins. Courtesy of the Canadian Museum of Civilization, No. 51166.

and have children was viewed as a very unfortunate person. Most marriages were arranged by parents, often while their children were quite young. Girls were married at or just after puberty (probably fourteen to sixteen years of age). Males married somewhat later since they had to prove themselves capable of supporting a family, by hunting and fishing. With the population so widely scattered, it was not possible for young people to arrange their own marriages as is done today. Parents, with their more extensive networks and more knowledge about other families, were in a better position to choose partners for their children. However, children did have some veto power over these arrangements. Both Jenness and Stefansson described several instances in which a girl refused to marry the man chosen for her. As in all aspects of Copper Inuit life, there was flexibility in such negotiations. Although it was considered ideal for a man and woman to be approximately the same age (or at least the same generation), high death rates often forced people to marry individuals considerably older or younger than themselves. The high death rate (from hunting accidents and starvation) resulted in many people marrying several times in the course of a lifetime. The harshness of arctic conditions made it very difficult for people to stay married all their lives to the same individual. In addition, the scarcity of women due to the practice of selective female infanticide resulted in a certain amount of competition between men for wives.

The Hardship of the Old Days

Albert Palvik. I know of lots of times when parents had to leave their children out on the ice—when there were hard times. This happened even when I was growing up. They would wrap them up soon after they were born and leave them out on the land or on the ice. Mostly the boys were kept. For that reason, there are a lot of families with no relatives left anymore. They just died out.

Agnes Nigiyok. When I started to wake up, my adoptive parents would tell me stories about the past. I was born during the spring down in Prince Albert Sound. I was adopted because my [biological] parents [Pituitok and Kupeuna] wanted to throw me away. They had put me into a caribou sling with a looped drawstring. And for my mouth, they had a mouthpiece ready for me. Then Nilgaks entered the tent [Nilgak and Annie Otoayok]. When they were told that my parents were going to throw me out.

These were relations to Otoayok [Otoayok was Kupeuna's sister]. When they said all that, Nilgak picked me up without hesitation right away from the skin that was for me. Otoayok could not bear any more children. That's when Nilgak had married her. Nilgak had married Otoayak even though she wasn't able to bear anymore children. They had had only one child—Akkowakiut—when they first got together.

When I was older [when she was perhaps nine or ten], I was taken away by Hikoaluks for a daughter-in-law. I was taken from my adoptive mother even though she didn't want them to take me. She told them that I was still too young and hadn't learned enough to be a wife. Hikoaluks told my adoptive mother that they would teach me all those things. Hikoaluks took me down around the Coppermine area. That summer, we traveled west of Coppermine hunting caribou and trapping. When winter came, we were near Pierce Point on the coast. That's when I was left behind, on a big bay near Pierce Point. I don't know why I was left behind. I tried really hard. Maybe it was because I didn't know how to sew very well or do anything because I was too young. Sewing is hard when you first leave your family. It's very hard. I hadn't even sewn my first pair of mitts. I was just a young girl then. When they left me, I came near freezing. It was during the winter and I was left out on the ice. My body was partly frozen, but just on the surface—the skin on some parts of my body. My feet weren't so bad. I kept on walking. I walked all the way on the ice to the land following their trail. I tried not to lose their trail. The daylight was short. The day was over so soon. It must have been around December. I would cry every so often, then start on the trail again. I would find a snowhouse and enter, but there would be nothing inside. Not even a piece of meat. They wouldn't even leave a piece of food for me, and they knew that I was following their trail. There were two policemen and two Inuit who found me. The Inuit were Simon Bennett and Alex Lester. I don't remember the names of the policemen. That was the first time I saw white people. They took me to a place near Paulatuk where Inglanasaks and Ningasiks were camped. Before the day was out, I found out that Hikoaluks were at that camp too. Ningasiks took care of me and gave me clothes. They had to cut the clothes off my body because they were frozen so stiff. I stayed with them for about a year. Then Hikoaluks took me back, but left me again. After that, I was adopted by Lennie Inglangasak and his wife Sarah. They had a ship. Lennie was a trapper and we would spent year to year at different places.

Frank Kuptana. A long time ago, there were people living in Prince Albert Sound. One year, the ice broke up early and the people ended up on the islands. Those people of long ago— old timers—were hunting seal. Some of them went out of their minds. They spent the summer there and ran out of food. They starved. Unayak was an old man [when he told the story]. He told a lot of stories. Also Egyukhiak. Those people were slowly dying out until there was only one couple and their daughter left. They would chew on their caribou skins. The ducks finished nesting. The couple and their daughter started making a kayak to travel to the mainland. When they finished the kayak, the father and daughter traveled to the mainland, saying that they would come back for the wife. They were headed for Naudlat, but the current brought them to Qiqiqtaqyuak [Holman Island]. When they reached there, he caught a bull caribou with his bow and arrow. Then he wanted to go pick up his wife from the islands, but it was bad weather for a long time. So he never went to pick her up.

Rene Taipana. There were a lot of people long ago before there were any white men. It seems like people never got sick that often. And people came together from everywhere. Long ago, some of the people died due to illness, when they got very sick. The sickness in those days wasn't like the complicated illnesses of today. It was said and known that people then rarely got sick.

Sam Oliktoak. But people would die of starvation. My mother's father, when he was still alive, said that a lot of people died one winter. The weather wasn't good. They ran out of food. They starved to death. That's how a lot of people died too. Back then, they had no stores to buy food from. Bad weather. People didn't go out hunting much that winter. They ran out of food and died. That's when my mother's father was living yet.

Marriages occurred without a formal ceremony. A man and woman simply took up residence with one another and assumed the roles of husband and wife. A period of bride-service was often required for one to two years. During this time, a young man was expected to live and travel with his bride's family. Once the couple was considered mature enough, they could embark on their own. The period of bride-service thus represented a form of trial marriage, allowing the couple to grow into adult roles with some parental supervision. Not all marriages were preceded by bride-service, however. In cases where the bride and/or groom were older, marrying perhaps for a second time, bride-service might not be required at all. In other situations, a valued item might be given by the groom to the bride's father, the gift taking the place of bride-service (see Damas 1975).

Although there was a fairly distinct division of labor by sex, there was also sufficient flexibility in gender-based activities than an individual of one sex could perform activities of the opposite sex without incurring social scorn or condemnation. Women were generally in charge of sewing, skin preparation, cooking, and household duties, while men were responsible for hunting and maintaining hunting and traveling equipment.

Partnerships and Alliances

The Copper Inuit maintained a large number of formal and informal partnerships that were designed to create special bonds of affection and/or support among nonrelatives, actually maintaining a greater number of such relationships than neighboring Inuit groups. Given the fact that kinsmen were often widely dispersed throughout much of the year, and certainly did not reside together on a permanent basis, there was a great need to establish close working relations with unrelated families upon whom one might come to depend for assistance.

The most ubiquitous form of partnership was the seal-sharing partnership discussed above. Perhaps more dramatic and more widely known were the spouse exchange relationships. Such a strong bond was established between exchanging couples that even their children were considered brothers and sisters, and thus prohibited from marrying one another. Spouse exchanges could occur only once for a short duration or could be initiated on multiple occasions for varying lengths of time. Jenness (1922:86) notes that such relationships were often established when a family visited a group that contained no kinsmen or partners. Once an exchange was arranged, however, the newly arrived family ceased to be considered strangers and could thus easily interact with other members of the group. Jenness observes that spouse exchanges were also arranged between couples who normally resided in the same region, and that such exchanges typically occurred when the two couples came together again after a prolonged separation. Other partnerships important in Copper Inuit society included dancing partnerships, joking relationships, and namesake partnerships. All of these alliances were initiated to help create bonds of affection and mutual support between individuals. Joking partnerships (*kipaqatigiik*), for example, involved good-natured sarcasm, irony, and banter; and in the case of cross-sex joking relationships there was erotic suggestiveness and horseplay (see Damas 1971:45). There is some indication that joking partners may also have become involved in spouse-exchange relationships.

A common practice among many Inuit groups was (and continues to be) the passing of names down from one generation to the next. Several special kinds of relationships were created through this tradition. First, a special bond was created between a deceased individual and the newborn named after him or her. This special relationship also extended to the relatives and close friends of the deceased individual. Another bond was created between individuals with the same name, whether or not they were related to one another. This was not a formal relationship, but might involve the periodic exchange of gifts.

Religion

As with many other Inuit groups, Copper Inuit religion was more concerned with the here and now than with an afterlife. Most important was the relationship between humans and the spirits of the animals upon which humans depended for food. It was essential that the proper rituals be followed, so as not to offend these spirits, who were perceived as being much like humans. An animal spirit that had been offended through the violation of a taboo or the omission of an important ritual might decide to take revenge upon the group as a whole. Illness, starvation, or some other disaster could result. The Copper Inuit observed a number of taboos which were believed to be important to maintaining good relations with the spirit world. A number of observances were related to the separation of land animals and sea animals. Copper Inuit were prohibited from cooking products of the land and sea in the same pot. Nor could they place seal meat next to caribou meat on the sleeping platform of the snowhouse. Most pronounced was the prohibition against sewing caribou skin clothing during the early winter. All winter clothing had to be prepared in the fall, at the gathering places, and completed before the move to the sealing grounds on the sea ice.

In addition to believing in the spirits of animals and the

shades of deceased humans, the Copper Inuit subscribed to a world inhabited by wondrous and often dangerous creatures: dwarfs, giants, and caribou people. They believed in a sea goddess (known as Sedna in other regions), who controlled the animals of the seas. Arnapkapfaaluk, or "big bad woman," was not a benevolent goddess looking out for human beings: when offended by the violation of a taboo or some indiscriminate action, she could withhold the seals upon which people depended for survival.

Animal Spirits

William Kuptana. The custom of the Eskimos is that when they take part in a hunt and make a kill, all who hunted the animal must participate in the cutting and sharing of the carcass. Those who do not follow that custom embarrass the animal spirit; therefore, it is believed that the nonparticipant will be hunted himself.

Death was not accompanied by elaborate ceremony. In winter, the body was usually left behind in a snowhouse, while in summer, the body was wrapped in skins and left on the tundra. The concept of an afterlife was not well developed. Jenness reported that it was definitely not viewed as a land of joy and plenty, but a "vague and gloomy realm where, even if want and misery are not found (and of this they are not certain), joy and gladness at least must surely be unknown." (Jenness 1922:190)

Shamans (*angatkut*) served as important intermediaries between humans and the spirit world. Shamans provided a number of essential functions. They could act as healers, in the event of an illness, or could determine what taboos were violated when animals became scarce. They were also believed to have powers for controlling the weather and warding off evil spirits. The shaman, acting as an intermediary, could communicate with animal spirits, often doing so with the aid of a spirit helper or familiar. Most angatkut claimed to have more than one helper. Jenness met one Copper Inuit shaman, Uloksak, who claimed to have a white man, a polar bear, a wolf, and a dog as helping spirits. Shamans could be either male or female, but no matter what their gender they were expected to have some kind of visionary experience whereby a spirit helper revealed itself to the future angatkut. In their shamanistic performances, shamans may have relied upon ventriloquism and other dramatic acts to impress their audiences and demonstrate their powers. Shamans by definition were neither good nor bad. Some angatkut developed reputations for kindness and generosity; others were greatly feared and used their powers to gain advantage over others.

Shamanism

William Kuptana. So then, when winter finally appeared, all the hunting parties gathered where they always gathered at this time. The places are called Umingmakyuk [Umingmagiuk] and Napirakvik [Napiragvik]. When the hunting parties gathered at the two adjacent places, the women would bolt into action by making caribou skin clothing for the rest of the clan. While waiting for the women to accomplish their tasks, the men resorted to shamanism. Anyone who was ill was cured quickly by a momentous action as if the disease itself was a substance to be taken out [of the body]. If that ill person breached, then they knew they were infringing upon the disease. Then it was bitten out of the ill person, so it seemed. But when a cure was not in sight, more shamans were called to cast out whatever vice was still in the ill person. Caribou mitts or caribou mukluks were given in return for a cure. For instance, shamans would take a knife and slice up a caribou mitt. The sliced up mitt would then be eaten by the participating shamans. When they had eaten the whole thing, one of them would grab a parka and shake it until a mitt dropped out. It was enthralling to see such a practice.

I've also been a spectator of one other such practice. My wife's grandfather would grow polar bear teeth sitting by the door of the snowhouse. He would start growling fervently. At one time, people had to tie him up because he got so strong they had to keep him at bay.

Kuptan, my namesake, was also a shaman. People were afraid of him. But at one time while they were hunting, they came upon a musk ox. So this shaman [Kuptan] blinded the musk ox, and the rest of the hunting part was able to kill it.

Tolerance and Forbearance

In conclusion, it can be said that, like other Canadian Inuit groups, the Copper Inuit were remarkable in their ability to adapt to a harsh and unforgiving environment. Through flexible social relations, an emphasis on cooperation and mutual support, and a sophisticated material technology, the Copper Inuit were able to survive and develop a viable and dynamic culture. Early explorers and anthropologists who made contact with the Copper Inuit during the period of initial contact were invariably impressed by their stoic demeanor and cheerful outlook on life. Laughter, irony, and a good sense of humour were considered to be valued characteristics. This included an uncanny ability for individuals to laugh at themselves in embarrassing social situations. The person who was not cheerful but gloomy and complaining was viewed as having a character flaw. This is easily understandable. The ability to laugh at all kinds of misfortune and hardship was a necessary ingredient for dealing with the uncertainties of a difficult northern life.

Traditional Copper Inuit Culture

A Hard Life

Frank Kuptana. When I started waking up, my family lived on the land at the end of Minto Inlet. My father was Iqalukpik, and when he died my mother remarried a man called Urhuraq. My stepfather was very mean to me. He was a man who would fight a lot. My mother used to feel sorry for me. She said that she got tired of feeling sorry for me. So when Urhuraq went fishing to a lake, that's when we left. He couldn't track us down since there was no more snow. I never did see him again. He must have looked for us, but he never did find us. My mother must have known that there were people down around Read Island, so that's where we ran off to. I remember that we traveled until we reached a river—Kuujjuak [Kuugyuaq]. We must have been way inland. We traveled across the river. I remember when we crossed the river, because when she crossed it, my mother was crying. I fed from her breast after we crossed it. That's when I was still being packed. A sealskin pouch with her needle, thread, and ulu, and sealskin material for patches for her shoes—those were the only things that my mother carried. I remember when she had me stick my head out of her hood while packing me. Sometimes I forget parts of my life, and some parts I remember as though I am so smart. I remember my mother crying. Eventually, we reached people around Read Island—a place called Ippiulik. That's where we met some people. There were quite a few people there—Kanayoks and Qiyuliuts. Qiyuliut's wife was Qiqhaq and Qunmuktuk was their son. My mother and I were adopted by Kanayoks and those people looked after us. Then, my mother married Qunmuktuk.

After this Qunmuktuk became my stepfather, we started traveling around on the island near Coppermine. That man Qunmuktuk was a very nice man. He sure was good to me. He showed me a lot of affection. He never scolded me. He sure was a good man. That's how I remember him. It was with him that I grew up to be a young boy. We lived on a big body of land, the land of the Coppermine area. We spent the summer where there are caribou. We packed what we needed on our backs. We would pack our camping gear, and the dogs would carry the tents on both sides.

We lived around Coppermine for a while. I grew up to be a young boy around Coppermine. That's the furthest place we ran off to, and that's where we hunted caribou throughout the summer and fall. Then my stepfather Qunmuktuk died. My mother remarried a man called Uikiaq. My mother and Qunmuktuk never had any children. I know that. My mother was sick throughout the summer and winter. Her body was pretty much finished from the sickness. She died around Read Island, while she was with her last husband Uikiaq. After that, I stayed with Uikiaq. He had a son called Qahapina. I stayed with them— trapping. It was with Uikiaq and Qahapina that I grew up to be a fine young man.

Early chroniclers of Copper Inuit culture were also impressed with their energy, patience, and endurance. As Jenness (1922:235) wrote:

> The Copper Eskimos think nothing of spending twenty-four hours on a hunt, tramping continually over stony hills without a morsel of food, and with only a few short halts to rest their limbs and look around them. In spring I have seen them spend whole days fruitlessly digging one hole after another through the thick ice of the lakes and jigging their lines without ever getting a bite. In winter they sit for hours over their seal-holes even in howling blizzards with the temperature 30 and more below zero Fahrenheit. The patience instilled in them by hunting becomes so engrained in their very natures and permeates all their social life, so that tolerance and forbearance are two of the most marked features in Eskimo society.

4. Trappers, Traders, and Transitional Copper Inuit Culture

WITH THE COLLAPSE of the commercial whale fishery around 1906, large numbers of whalers turned to trapping and trading to make a living. Former whalers, such as Joseph Bernard, Christian T. Pedersen, William Mogg, Christian Klengenberg, William Seymour, Fritz Wolki, and others, began trading with the Inuit, first from their ships, which wintered over in strategic locations, and later from permanent trading posts. The first permanent trading posts in Copper Inuit territory were not established until 1916. In that year, the Hudson's Bay Company (HBC) opened a post (Fort Bacon) at Bernard Harbor and Klengenberg built a post south of Cape Kendall, near the mouth of the Coppermine River. In 1919, Klengenberg relocated his post to Rymer Point on the southwest coast of Victoria Island. After 1920, this post operated in the name of his daughter Etna and her husband, Ikey Bolt, an Inuk from Point Barrow, Alaska.

The Arrival of Traders

Albert Palvik. When the traders came up here, it really affected our way of life and trading. The trading post had wood, knives, rifles, and steel axes, so people stopped trading among themselves. When the trading posts came, it affected our way of hunting too. We got rifles so we did not have to travel as far or

91

Fig. 4.1. *Bear Tracks*, Holman Print Collection, 1992. Woodcut by Mary Okheena (artist) and Susie Malgokak (printer). Edition: 35. Courtesy of the Holman Eskimo Cooperative.

work as hard to get food. We still hunted seals using harpoons. In those days, we lived mainly on caribou in the summertime. When we got rifles, we did not have to go as far from the trading post to get caribou. But people still traveled a lot though.

When the traders came around, they wanted foxes. They would give us rifles, shells, and traps. I got my first rifle from the traders when I was still living in Prince Albert Sound. The traders at Halahiqvik [Fort Brabant] used to send some Inuit workers to different camps with rifles, knives, and traps so we could go out and trap foxes. Some of Charlie Klengenberg's sons, like Andy, would travel around and give rifles and other supplies. It must have been in the 1920s. Captain Charlie [Klengenberg] used to travel with his daughter who would translate for him. When Captain Charlie and his sons were traveling to the camps, it was more convenient to trade with him rather than go to the HBC trading post at Halahiqvik. He usually traveled here by sled in the winter, coming up from around the Coppermine area. That's where the Klengenbergs settled and started their trading posts.

In the next fifteen years there was intense competition between the small independent traders and large companies such as HBC. The Bay received significant competition from the Klengenbergs, L. F. Semmler, and Pedersen's Canalaska Trading Company, all of which operated chains of trading posts. Usher (1965) notes that at least fifty-one different posts were established at one time or another in the area, (most of them, however, were south of the Holman region, in Coronation Gulf or Dolphin and Union Straits). The struggle for dominance in the region was an intense one, but by 1950, the Hudson's Bay Company had either bought out or put out of business all its competitors. Klengenberg and Pedersen were both bought out by the Bay and by the late 1940s the Semmler posts had failed. Usher (1965:51–52) notes:

> By 1950, "The Bay" had triumphed completely, primarily because of its greater size and ability to withstand the losses incurred by such disasters as bad fox years, bad ice years when supply vessels could not get in, or even the loss of a supply vessel. However, the fact that the company had had to operate posts at fourteen different locations during that time bears witness to the ferocity of the struggle. . . . Another factor which brought the free trader era to a close was the conservation legislation introduced in 1938, which was designed to preserve the game for the exclusive use of the native peoples. . . . Most if not all of the free traders could not survive without also trapping and hunting. With the privilege denied, no more entered the country, and it was then only a matter of time before the white trappers already there either died or retired from the north.

While such conditions probably helped to put a number of white traders out of business, the restrictions did not affect traders of mixed descent, most notably the Klengenberg sons and daughters, who continued hunting, trapping, and trading throughout Copper Inuit territory. The failure of the native trading posts was probably more a result of undercapitalization and insufficient resources compared with the powerful, wealthy Hudson's Bay Company. The trading post of Lena Klengenberg at Cape Krusenstern closed down in 1936; that of Ikey Bolt and Etna Klengeberg at Rymer Point closed in 1937 (Usher 1965:54–55).

The first post in the Holman region was opened by the Hudson's Bay Company in 1923, at Halahiqvik, on the north shore of Prince Albert Sound. Named Fort Brabant, after Angus Brabant, who was the HBC fur trade commissioner between 1920 and 1927, it was extremely small. It was also the northernmost trading post in Copper Inuit territory. Written records of the post's early years appear to have been destroyed in a fire and the earliest surviving documentation is the Fort Brabant journal of 1927/1928, which notes that the supply ship arrived on August 26 to find the "dwelling house with all the books burned down." There is no further clarification as to what happened to the post building or to the journals. Holman elder Esau Elgayak remembers that a fire devastated the post, but he does not know how it started. He notes that all the people who hunted and trapped in that area moved away after the fire.

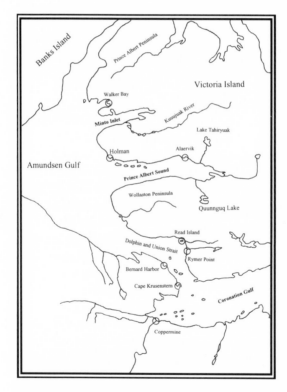

Alaervik (Halahaqvik):	
HBC (Fort Brabant)	1923–1928
Bernard Harbor:	
HBC (Fort Bacon)	1916–1932
Cape Krusenstern:	
L. Klengenberg	1926–1936
HBC	1926–1929
William Seymour	1927–1933
Canalaska Trading Co.	1932–1934
L. F. Semmler	1932–1946
Coppermine:	
C. Klengenberg	1916–1923
HBC	1928–present
Catholic Mission	1929–1950
L. F. Semmler	1933–1935
Holman:	
HBC	1939–present
Catholic Mission	1943–1950
Read Island:	
Canalaska Trading Co.	1931–1938
HBC	1931–1962
L. F. Semmler	1938–1948
Rymer Point:	
C. Klengenberg	1919–1928
HBC (Fort Harmon)	1923–1927
Ikey Bolt/E. Klengenberg	1932–1937
Walker Bay:	
HBC (Fort Collinson)	1928–1939
Canalaska Trading Co.	1932–1938

Map 9. Location of major trading posts in the Holman-Coppermine region, Northwest Territories. Between 1916 and the early 1940s, at least fifty-one trading posts were in operation in the Holman-Coppermine region. Only those trading posts mentioned in the text are shown here.

Fishing at Kuuk

Frank Kuptana. My Mom died around Read Island. I heard that my mother came from the Cambridge Bay area. That's where she lived first. In those days, people would travel back and forth from Cambridge Bay to Prince Albert Sound, going across the land. In Prince Albert Sound, there was a post, and a clerk by the name of Millak [Miller?] used to work there. He was a white man. Also, they had Emerak working with that clerk back then. Now, only an icehouse is left there. That icehouse belonged to the HBC post. Back then, there were a lot of fish in the inlet so people liked to go to the end of Prince Albert Sound to fish. There is a river where people would build fish weirs in the summer and fish. That's where people would set their fish weirs and fish. The river Kuuk. That's where they got lots of fish.

Fort Brabant was not a busy post, even after being rebuilt. The lone HBC manager, R. L. Miller, wrote that he did not receive his first Inuit visitors until November 15, almost three months after his arrival by boat (Fort Brabant Journal, 1927–1928). That winter, most of the Inuit of Prince Albert Sound had gone northwest to Banks Island and Minto Inlet, where hunting conditions were better. The only family near the post was that of Fred Kahak's father, Numareena (Nomagina). Later, in the spring, business picked up as Inuit arrived from Banks Island to trade fox skins. By and large, trapping had not yet become an important part of the Copper Inuit economy. Most of the Copper Inuit of western Victoria Island still followed a relatively seasonal round of hunting and fishing. The HBC manager wrote: "No one is trapping except for tobacco and ammunition" (Fort Brabant Journal, 1927/1928). Manager Miller also discovered that many of the Inuit were saving about half their foxes to trade with Ikey Bolt at Rymer Point.

The journal mentions the names and activities of only a handful of Inuit. After spending the winter near the Fort Brabant post, Numareena and his family left on May 14 for their summer camp on the south shore of Prince Albert Sound. Two families, however, remained at the post to work over the summer. These are identified in the journal as the families of Kahak (possibly Fred Kahak) and Neloona (Neroona?). According to Nichol Uluariuk, Mark Emerak (who later established a reputation as one of Holman's finest artists) also worked at the Fort Brabant post, but probably several years before the fire.

95

Fig. 4.2. Fort Brabant (HBC) post, Halahiqvik (Alaervik), north shore
of Prince Albert Sound. Fort Brabant was the first trading post located
directly in the Holman region. It opened in 1923 and was relocated
to Walker Bay in 1928. At the time of its opening, Fort Brabant was the
northernmost trading post in Copper Inuit territory. The photograph
shows both the store and the manager's residence circa 1925 before
the dwelling house burned down. Courtesy of Hudson's Bay Company
Archives, Provincial Archives of Manitoba, Photo A.102/1044/11, Neg.
No. N7100.

It was clear that most of the Inuit of Prince Albert Sound
had moved to Minot Inlet and Banks Island and HBC decided
to relocate to the north.[1] On August 22, 1928, the schooner
Aklavik arrived to move the Fort Brabant post from Prince Albert Sound to Walker Bay. The new post was built near the
location where Collinson had spent the winter of 1851/1852
aboard the *Enterprise*. A new manager, C. V. Rowan, was put
in charge. According to the 1928 Annual Report of the Western
Arctic District:

> Fort Brabant (henceforth to be called Fort Collinson) was moved
> in August 1928 from its former location on Prince Albert Sound
> to Walker Bay on the west coast of Victoria Island, where it was
> hoped that we should be in more convenient proximity to the
> hunting grounds of the natives. A successful year's trade has been
> done resulting in a net profit of $20,000, but at the close of the
> outfit, the majority of the natives with whom we traded migrated
> southwards, owing mainly to the scarcity of deer on Banks Island

1. Usher (1971:38) indicates that the Bay's decision to relocate was due
primarily to a change in government policy. In 1927, the government decided
that post licences would be issued for only three locations on the western
Arctic islands: Walker Bay, Cambridge Bay, and King William Island. The
government requested that the Bay close down its trading post in Prince
Albert Sound and relocate to Walker Bay.

Trappers, Traders, and Transitional Culture

Fig. 4.3. Hudson's Bay Company post, Walker Bay. Photo by Mrs. Peter Sidney. Courtesy of the National Archives of Canada, No. C38543, and of Peter Sidney and family.

and in the vicinity of Walker Bay. Consequently, it is anticipated that results of outfit 260 (1929–1930) will demonstrate the necessity of removing the post again in Prince Albert Sound.

The Inuit who traded with the HBC during the post's first year at Fort Collinson urged that the post be moved back to Prince Albert Sound. The manager noted that "all the people will be leaving here and not coming back . . . but if we erect a post in Prince Albert Sound, they will continue to trade with us" (Fort Collinson Journal, 1929, B405a). Rowan also learned that Numareena had two hundred foxes cached down in Prince Albert Sound and wanted to buy a house.

Despite the appeal by Prince Albert Sound people to move the post, the Bay decided to remain at Fort Collinson. In 1932, a competing company, Pedersen's Canalaska Trading Company, opened a post about nine miles to the southeast of the HBC post. In charge of this new post was a man named Chitty (first name not identified) assisted by William Kuptana, a Copper Inuk. The competition worked to the advantage of the local trappers. The Bay's policy until then had been to charge for all traps but when the HBC manager learned that the Canalaska post was lending traps to the Inuit he was forced to do the same (Fort Collinson Journal: November 8, 1932). A friendly rivalry soon developed between the Bay and the Canalaska post and during Christmas 1932 manager Rowan put on a large feast, apparently to create goodwill and encourage the Inuit to trade with the Bay. The Canalaska manager, who was included among the guests, used the occasion himself to encourage the Inuit to trade with him.

97

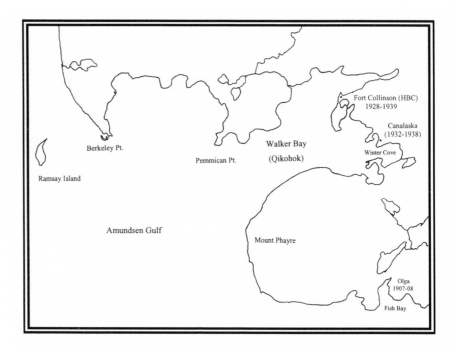

Map 10. The map shows Walker Bay and the location of Fort Collinson (HBC) store and the Canalaska Trading Company store. The stores competed for the Inuit trade. In 1938, the Canalaska Trading Company was bought out by the Hudson's Bay Company. In 1939, the Bay relocated its post to what is now King's Bay on the north shore of the mouth of Prince Albert Sound (not shown).

Fig. 4.4. Canalaska Trading Company post at Walker Bay. Holman elders identify the ship in the background as being the *Blue Fox*. Photo by Mrs. Peter Sidney. Courtesy of the National Archives of Canada, No. PA38541, and of Peter Sidney and family.

Arrival of the Western Inuit (Walliningmiut)

Although Walker Bay was located in the northernmost regions of Copper Inuit territory, it was far from being isolated. The two trading posts not only attracted Copper Inuit from Prince Albert Sound, Minto Inlet, and Banks Island, but also served as a trading center for western Inuit, who were primarily people of mixed white-Inuit ancestry and/or North Alaskan/Mackenzie Delta descent. These westerners, or Bankslanders as they would later be called, had only recently been attracted to the rich trapping grounds of Banks Island from the Mackenzie Delta region.

Prior to the introduction of trapping in the western Arctic, Banks Island had been used as a hunting ground solely by the Copper Inuit of Minto Inlet and Prince Albert Sound. Beginning in the late 1920s, however, Inuit trappers from the Mackenzie Delta began traveling to Banks Island for winter hunting and trapping. These Banks Island trappers soon became the first truly affluent Inuit in all of the Arctic. Since fox prices were at an all-time high in the 1920s, these trappers were able to purchase their own schooners and load them with supplies. On Banks Island, the schooners were hauled ashore, and the winter was spent trapping from base camps, made up of tents banked with sod. After break-up, the Banks Island schooners returned to the Delta loaded with furs.

One of the first and best known of these Banks Island trappers was Natkusiak, the guide who had been Stefansson's primary companion on his two northern expeditions (1908 to 1912 and 1913 to 1918). From 1914 to 1916, the northern party of the Canadian expedition had a permanent base camp at a location named Mary Sachs to the east of Cape Kellet, on southwestern Banks Island (approximately six miles west of the modern community of Sachs Harbour). It was from this camp that Stefansson, Natkusiak, and others in the group embarked on their extensive travels. During the winter of 1914/1915, a number of expedition members began trapping white fox on the side (Usher 1971:36). Apparently, foxes were plentiful in the immediate vicinity of the camp and large numbers of them were easily caught.

Natkusiak

Agnes Goose. My Dad [Natkusiak] used to work for Stefansson when he was traveling around here. His first wife was Kaudluak

Fig. 4.5. Natkusiak (Billy Banksland) and family at Walker Bay, circa 1935. Photo by Charles Rowan/Courtesy of NWT Archives.

from Coppermine. That was his first wife. Then he married my mother, Topsy Ikiuna. Her family was also working for Stefansson, and she and my Dad met up at Melville Island. After my Dad finished working for Stefansson, he lived on Banks Island and then moved to Baillie Island where they had a house. That's also when they adopted Jimmy [Memogana]. When my Dad finished working for Stefansson, he got the *North Star*. It was an old ship and eventually was wrecked when I was about seven years old. I remember seeing it when the waves took the boat, so I ran into the house and was crying. Someone had been using the boat to get driftwood and hadn't anchored it properly. So when it got really stormy, the waves just took the ship.

When I turned about eight years old [approximately 1933], my parents and us all moved to Banks Island. That spring, the ice kept us from going back [to the mainland]. So my Dad brought us here [to Victoria Island] because he knew this land very well. He had traveled here while working with Stefansson. He traveled all over and knew all about this land. So he brought us here by schooner. We came aboard somebody else's boat because our boat had been crushed to pieces at Baillie Island. We traveled here to Ulukhaktok on the *Shamrock,* on Fred Bennett Ningasik's boat. That's when I was seven years old. We spent the winter here [approximately 1933/1934]. There were other ships here too—the *Blue Fox* and the *Nanuk.* In the spring, my Dad and all of us went to Walker Bay to David Pirktuqana's [Piktukana's] to work on his schooner, the *Sea Otter*. We traveled up to Walker Bay by sled and dogs while the ice was still good. And then the summer came with the David Pirktuqana's and we sailed to Tuk. We then came back to Walker Bay. The David Pirktuqanas traveled off after some time, leaving us at Walker Bay. That time, we stayed on at Walker Bay. The next summer, the Pirktuqanas came back. They must have been in and around the Read Island area. Then, we traveled back to Tuk. That's about when David Bernhardt married my sister [Mary Nerlek]. David bought a ship called the *Okpik* and used that to travel back and forth to Banks Island from Tuk. That's when we started traveling with David Bernhardt.

We used to stay for a while up at Walker Bay where my Dad had a frame tent near the Canalaska post. We must have stayed up there for about a year. My Dad used to trap and work on and off for the Canalaska post with George Porter. Then my Dad was getting older, so we moved down here to Ulukhaktok to live. We came here and made this place our home when my brother George was two years old. Sometime around 1937. There were no posts here. The posts were still up at Walker Bay. We spent about two years here, then the posts moved down here. There were no people here at all back then.

At the end of the Canadian Arctic Expedition, Natkusiak was given one of the expedition's schooners, the *North Star*, as payment for his services. Natkusiak and a number of other Inuit who had worked for the expedition remained on Banks Island, trapping foxes for four winters. By the time they left in 1921, aboard the *North Star*, they had caught approximately one thousand white foxes (Usher 1971:37). But although this established the productivity of Banks Island, it was not until 1928 that other Inuit headed for these trapping grounds. As long as the trapping was good on the mainland, there was no need to look elsewhere for arctic foxes. By the late 1920s, however, significant overharvesting had reduced the number of mainland white foxes. There was also increased competition from white trappers; hence, three Inuit-owned schooners headed to Banks Island in the summer of 1928. Conveniently for the native people, the Canadian government in 1920 had designated Banks Island as a game preserve, reserved for Inuit only, in the same way that Victoria Island had been designated two years earlier. The regulations were designed to keep out an expected wave of white and native trappers from Alaska. The three schooners that made the first crossing were owned by the families of Lennie Inglangasak, David Pektukana (Pirktuqana), and Adam Inoalayak, with his son Paul. The trappers and their families spent the winter of 1928/1929 camped at the old base camp of the Canadian Arctic Expedition at Mary Sachs (Usher 1971:39–40). On the mainland, it was a bad trapping year, but these three families did moderately well, with over one hundred foxes each. In later years, increasing numbers of Inuit wintered on Banks Island, usually returning to Herschel Island (and later Aklavik) in summer to trade.

Throughout the 1930s and 1940s, the Banks Island schooner fleet increased in size. Most trading was done on the mainland, but a number of schooners began trading into Walker Bay, at either the Hudson's Bay post or the Canalaska post. In 1933/1934, a number of these westerners who had gone to Walker Bay to trade were unable to return to Banks Island due to heavy ice conditions. As a result, they wintered on Victoria Island and discovered that white foxes were as abundant there as they were on Banks Island (Usher 1971:52). Thereafter, some of these westerners continued to winter at various locations on western Victoria Island. Those who continued to favor Banks Island also made occasional midwinter and spring dog-sledding trips to Walker Bay, to trade and socialize. Meanwhile, the Copper Inuit continued to travel and hunt on Banks Island, coming into contact periodically with the western trappers. The Copper Inuit were still oriented more toward subsistence hunting, rather than intensive trapping.

Natkusiak, after dividing his time between Banks Island and Baillie Island, eventually moved with his family to the vicinity of Walker Bay, and later to Holman. (One of Natkusiak's sons claims that Natkusiak and his family moved to Holman several years before the HBC post and the Roman Catholic Mission were established there in 1939.)

Natkusiak was a frequent visitor to both the HBC post and the Canalaska post. George Burnham, who was a Bay clerk at Fort Collinson during the winter of 1935, remembered him, writing:

Another of our "regulars" was Billie Banksland who was some-what taller than the usual Inuit. He had worked with the Stefansson Expedition of 1914–1917 and was very well known and highly respected all along the coast. One of his favorite tricks on meeting someone "new" was to dress up in a complete outfit of polar bear skin, sneak up behind the unsuspecting stranger and grab him

Fig. 4.6. Egg River, Banks Island, meeting of western and Copper Inuit, spring 1932. The photographer, Mrs. Peter Sidney, was the wife of a Banks Island trapper. Beginning in the late 1920s, western Inuit trappers from the Mackenzie Delta started traveling to Banks Island on schooners to exploit the island's rich trapping grounds. Banks Island was also a traditional hunting territory for Copper Inuit from Minto Inlet and Prince Albert Sound. The two groups came into frequent contact with one another on Banks Island and at the Walker Bay trading posts. Note the Alaskan-style basket sled in the foreground. Photo by Mrs. Peter Sidney. Courtesy of the National Archives of Canada, No. PA27690, and of Peter Sidney and family.

in a big bear hug. Naturally the visitor would look down to see who or what was holding him and all he would see would be what appeared to be the feet of a bear—imagine his surprise and shock! Billie would then release his captive and burst into loud laughter accompanied by whoever else was present (Burnham 1986:129–130).

Another westerner who traded into the Walker Bay posts at this time was David Bernhardt (son of the white fur trader Frank Bernhardt). Others included Alex Stefansson (son of Vilhjalmur Stefansson), Luke Miliksuk and his son Mahook (Mashook), Johnny "Onearm" Togluk, Fred Wolki, David Pektukana (Pirktuqana), Gerard and William Siksigaluk (Sixiealuk), Peter and Johnny Norberg, Andy Klengenberg, and George Avakana.

Shipwreck of the *Hazel*

Agnes Nigiyok. I only returned here [to Prince Albert Sound] after I had a child. I had been taken over to that side [the west]

103

Fig. 4.7. Johnny "Onearm" Togluk, Charles Rowan, and Gerard Siski-galuk (Sixealuk) in front of HBC store at Walker Bay, 1934 or 1935. Photo Courtesy of George Burnham, Winnipeg.

when I was still small. After I was over there for a while, I married. I was living with my adoptive parents, Lennie and Sarah Inglana-sak. When I was ready to get married, they had me marry some-one from farther to the west, someone from Alaska. My hus-band's name was Jacob Nipalakyok [Nipalariuk]. He was born around North Pole, Alaska, while his parents were trapping. After we were married, we lived together around Paulatuk, Letty Har-bor, Baillie Island, and at Aklavik. One summer, we went to Baillie Island when the ship carrying the supplies for all the stores came. Right now, there's no more people living there. We called Baillie Island Utqaluk. During that time, ships would come from the west to Baillie Island. There were people coming from the far west to go trapping around here.

There was an Inuinnaq couple there. It was Johnny "One Arm" Togluk and his wife and two children. They were getting ready to go to the posts at Walker Bay to do some trading. Togluk knew about my adoptive mother, Annie Otoayok, who was still living in Prince Albert Sound. After hearing this news about my adoptive mother still being alive, Jacob really wanted to come back over here. We were grateful that we had taken our dogs over to Baillie Island. Togluk had a fair-sized boat, but the engine on that boat was not very good. There were a lot of people who wanted to cross over to Banks Island and Walker Bay. The Togluks wanted to take us back here, so we went with them. When we got on the boat, it was like we were traveling someplace far. We got on the ship with our Aunt Panigabluk and David Bernhardt. There were six of us. David had spent the winter with Natkusiaks at Walker Bay. That was the only ship going from Baillie Island to this way. The engine kept on breaking down so only the sail was keeping it going. It was becoming winter and getting colder and colder. The top of the deck was covered with ice—even our dogs. The dogs were on the top deck of the ship. We went through quite a few days with white caps in the ocean, and it snowed. It was cold. It was quite a few days to cross over to Prince Albert Sound. The ship was really going from side to side. The waves were very high. The men who were steering the boat weren't eating much because they were trying to keep it afloat. My husband told me that they could see land, but they didn't know what place it was. I couldn't recognize the land either. It must have been around where I grew up, but I couldn't remember. I returned down to where my daughter was sleeping. She was two years old at the time [approximately 1934].

My husband called me up again to tell me that we were reaching the land. We were reaching the land very quickly. Togluk went to the sail and cut all the ropes. There were ice floes along the shore. The waves came up over the ship so there was no place for us to stand. I could hear the bottom of the ship hitting against the rocks. My husband called me and told us to get out from inside the ship. He told me to take the cover and thick blanket and to put my daughter on my back. I also went and got my husband's tobacco pouch. The ship was getting full of water. I didn't know how we were going to get on the land. We were reaching along the shore. There were two big logs in between the ice floes. Nipalakyok and David brought them to the ship to use them to go where it's shallow. The ship was starting to sink because of all the load. The load prevented it from getting closer to the shore. The coals must have been weighing down the ship. When we reached a shallow area, they tied a log onto the shore so it wouldn't float away. We tried to get Panigabluk to go on the first log, but she wouldn't do it. She wanted me to go to the land first. It was cold, so when I got out of the water, my clothes quickly froze. The land was covered with snow. There was white out all over the land. When they brought the log back to the ship to get Panigapluk, the log broke just when she was going to get on it. Thank God for the second log. They used the second log to bring her back to the land. They brought some other stuff to the land as well. Whenever they were able to get off the log, they would wade the rest of the way to shore. I asked myself, "how are we going to dry our clothes—how are we going to dry ourselves?"

Where we went on the land, there was an old campsite and some old logs around that could be used for firewood. That area must have been used during the summer by people from Prince Albert Sound or Read Island. I was very thankful for the firewood that was already cut. But we didn't know where to stay. We didn't have any tent or shelter. It was all gravel where we were and it was all covered with snow. After we were on the land, we made a fire. Then it started to get calm and it stopped snowing. I was glad that I had brought the tent and the blanket on the deck of the ship because they eventually drifted to the shore. Those were some of the few things that drifted ashore. All our dogs but one made it to the shore. Only one of them froze. We didn't have much to eat. If we didn't have our tent, we probably would have all frozen to death. We made a big fire inside the tent and dried the clothes that were wet.

After we were there wandering around for a while, David Bernhardt and my husband found an old kayak that was covered with bearded-seal skin. We were able to fix it up and use it to hunt seals along the shore. We were also able to retrieve one of the rifles from the shipwreck, and there was ammunition in the suitcase that Nipalakyok brought to shore with him. That's how we were able to feed ourselves.

When the lakes along the shore got ice, Johnny Togluk and David Bernhardt walked to Read Island to get Togluk's dogs. Togluks had left their dogs there for the summer. When they got their dogs, they came back to pick up Togluk's wife, and the three of them traveled up to Walker Bay. The two of us and Panigabluk stayed behind because there wasn't room on the sleds for everybody. We knew that, once Togluk told people where we were, people would come to pick us up. Shortly after Christmas, Simon Bennett and Dennis Avakana came by dogsled to pick us up. When we came this way, we didn't come to Uluk-haktok. There were no people living here then. We went up to Minto Inlet. We traveled up to Kuujjuak where we found lots of people camped: Kuniluk and his parents, Bennetts, Elunaks [Rosie Qiuvikhak's parents], and Emeraks. My adoptive mother

Otoayok was there too, She was very old. I also met her second husband Nokalalok. I never thought that I would see her again. She died about two years later.

After that, we traveled around Minto Inlet and Prince Albert Sound with different people. We wanted to move back across to Paulatok where all our belongings were, but Nipalakyok didn't want to cross over by dog-team and we had no other way to get across. We moved to Ulukhaktok when they moved the post down here from Walker Bay. My husband used to work on and off for the Bay doing odd jobs.

In many respects, the trading posts at Walker Bay provided the stage for a meeting between two quite different Inuit cultures. The westerners were much more economically acculturated than the resident Copper Inuit. Many, such as Natkusiak, were of Alaskan descent, while others had fathers who were white whalers who took Canadian Inuit wives. Others, such as Andy Klengenberg, were of both European and Alaskan descent. The Copper Inuit, on the other hand, had much more limited experience with the outside world. While the westerners had become fairly active trappers early on, and when fur prices were at their height, the Copper Inuit of western Victoria Island took longer to get so involved in the trapping economy. During most of the 1920s and 1930s, much of their traditional subsistence cycle was still oriented toward hunting and fishing, and they did only as much trapping as was necessary to get a few valued trade goods. Peter Usher notes:

Because traders did not penetrate the study area [Coppermine-Holman region] until the latter days of the fur boom, and because at first the Eskimos were grossly underpaid for their furs, two significant differences arose between the Copper Eskimos and the Mackenzie Delta people who had been in contact with the traders for some decades previous. There did not arise in the study area a generation of really excellent Copper Eskimo trappers, because there had been less opportunity for them to learn the trade during the peak trapping years. Secondly, in the Mackenzie Delta, where the trappers had received top prices for the furs in the 1920s, the people amassed capital goods on a large scale. Some of these goods, such as schooners, remain in the area to this day [1965], and continue to be of benefit. This capitalization on the part of the Eskimos never took place in the study area, and while the Copper Eskimos did not suffer the same descent from opulence that the Delta people did, neither did they receive any of the benefits from that era (Usher 1965:98).

One reason for the intense competition between trading companies in the Copper Inuit region was that the stakes were so high, especially since it was possible to take advantage of people who had limited experience with trapping and trading. Many of the traders engaged in dubious trading practices. The Inuit were often cheated. Godsell (1934:273) reports that in 1923 a white fox skin sold for $40 at the fur auction in London, while an Inuk from the Coppermine-Holman region was expected to pay twenty pelts for a $25 Winchester rifle. Godsell is prone to great exaggeration in his writing, but there is no doubt that a number of traders were extremely exploitative. Individual trading records from the HBC's Fort Collinson post are not available for public scrutiny, and possibly the presence of the westerners and the competing Canalaska company may have modified these exploitative practices in the Walker Bay area.

As already mentioned, the westerners did not restrict their trapping activities to Banks Island. Beginning in the 1930s, the western trappers took their schooners deeper into Copper Inuit territory, setting up temporary trapping camps at Ulukhaktok, Anialik, and elsewhere. At these locations, and at the trading posts, the Copper Inuit and the westerners came into close contact with one another.

Not much is known about the nature of relations between the Copper Inuit and the westerners (the Walliningmiuk, as the local people called them) who were entering their territory. Stefansson observed that some of the western Inuit who accompanied him to Victoria Island made fun of the Copper Inuit, not only because their dialect was different but because they were perceived as being more primitive. At the same time, some westerners feared the Copper Inuit for their purported shamanistic abilities (Father Henri Tardy, personal communication). Rather than viewing the Copper Inuit as more primitive, people like Stefansson were more inclined to view them as uncorrupted by civilization. A similar view was expressed by a Roman Catholic missionary, Raymond de Coccala, who visited the people of Minto Inlet and Prince Albert Sound several times, beginning in the mid-1930s:

> To the Western and Eastern Eskimos, these people were known as the Krangmalit, derived from the word "kranga" meaning "beyond." All these groups spoke with a slightly different accent

from the Western and Eastern Eskimos. The former's distinguishing character was a smooth, less guttural manner of speech, wholly lacking the "s" sound which they replace with an aspirant "h." A more important difference between these groups and other Inuit was the energetic and more venturesome spirit, backed by a pleasanter disposition and a livelier native intelligence (de Coccala and King (1986:328).

Holman elders who remember their first contacts with the westerners, the Walliningmiut, report that they got along quite well with the newcomers. Although their dialect was slightly different, they were able to communicate easily with one another. Some of the Copper Inuit who traded into the Walker Bay area and who came into contact with the westerners (according to HBC records) included Igiukshiuk, Emerak, Kudluk, Kunilu, Kahak, Kataoyak, Pokuk, Nerriune, Pumyuk, Nappayuak, Povotak, Elongna, Macara, Kunana, Inuktalik, and Ilinnak.[2]

In areas where they shared camps, such as at Anialik and Kuujuak, they often socialized, playing games with one another, and HBC journals note that the westerners with schooners occasionally helped transport Copper Inuit families from their camps to the trading posts and back again. Sometimes, however, disagreements arose. One conflict involved a dispute between the Siksigaluk family and a Copper Inuit family. A young Copper Inuit girl who had been living with a Siksigaluk boy for most of the winter (most likely a trial marriage) had become pregnant. In the spring, the lad abandoned the girl and returned to his family. It happened that Frenchy Chartrand, the Royal Canadian Mounted Police (RCMP) constable from Coppermine, was making one of his rare patrols to Fort Collinson at the time and a hearing was convened. After both parties had testified, the policeman decided in favor of the girl's family and ordered the boy to give half of his winter fur trapping to the girl's father. This was acceptable to all parties, ending the dispute (Burnham 1986:116).

The presence of the westerners on northwest Victoria Island must have made a significant impression upon the Kangiryuarmiut and quite possibly helped facilitate the Kangiryuarmiut's gradual transition to trapping in the 1930s. Farquharson

2. All spellings provided here are according to Hudson's Bay Company documents. It is likely they are inaccurate. We have not altered these spellings, preferring to preserve the integrity of those records.

(1976:58) gives details of how the people of Minto Inlet made the transition from a traditional subsistence orientation to trapping:

> At first, most of the traplines were very short and ran along the coast. However, as desire for and dependence on trade good grew, and as the Minto people learned more about how to trap from the Western Inuit, they extended their trap lines far inland. People living at Berkeley Point, Boot Inlet, and Kuujjuak River directed their trap lines toward the H.B.C. and Canalaska Company posts near Walker Bay. Many of the western Inuit trapped from Holman east toward Kuuk River.

Contact with the western Inuit, especially those owning their own schooners, must have highlighted the wealth differences between the two groups. From the perspective of the Kangiryu-

Fig. 4.8. Ikey Bolt (center) and Albert Palvik (second from left) at Rymer Point, 1930. Ikey Bolt was a western Inuk who married Etna Klengenberg. Ikey and Etna operated the Rymer Point Trading post until 1937, when it closed. Even after the HBC established trading posts in Prince Albert Sound and Walker Bay, many Inuit from Prince Albert Sound preferred to trade with Ikey Bolt, who traveled widely throughout the Coppermine and Holman region. He adopted a young orphan, Matthew Malgokak, and raised him as a son. Malgokak eventually established a trapping camp at Berkeley Point. His family was among the last Inuit families to move into the newly created settlement of Holman. Photo by R. S. Finnie. Courtesy of the National Archives of Canada, No. PA100752.

armiut, the newcomers were indeed wealthy people. More importantly, they were fellow Inuit (though some were of mixed descent) in possession of items normally associated with white traders—rich men like Klengenberg and Pedersen. As elder Albert Palvik succinctly stated during a 1988 interview: "I remember those westerners. Those people used to come here to trap and trade. Some of them were pretty wealthy. They were able to buy lumber to build wood houses. They were mostly trappers, while the people around here were still mostly hunting and only doing a little bit of trapping."

The Westerners

Frank Kuptana. I remember meeting the westerners. Some of those people lived around Anialik and trapped around there. They had come up by ship. They had a house built also at Walker Bay. The westerners trapped there then. People who came by schooners. Sure a lot of people came up to trap. Long ago. That was before we all moved to Holman. I would see those westerners when we would gather together for Easter. They got along well with the people from around here. They seemed to get along right from when I first started seeing them.

Rene Taipana. The first trip that I made to Ulukhaktok was when there was no HBC post, only people from the West—Walliningmuit. They had come here by ship to trap during the trapping season—over from Tuktoyaktuk. There was only one ship. It was Pirktuqana's [Piktukana's] ship [the *Sea Otter*]. The rest of the people they were traveling with [other schooners from the Delta] must have stopped over at Banks Island. That's when the posts were up at Walker Bay. That first trip to Ulukhaktok was at Eastertime. There were some people from the west and also some Kangiryuartiaqmiut [people from Minto Inlet] came to have Easter here. We got along well with one another. We played games and had fun. We were able to understand one another fairly well.

Trading Post Life

For the HBC and Canalaska traders, life at the posts could often be extremely boring. Days or even weeks would go by without anyone arriving to trade. When a trapper did arrive, trading

111

would not commence until after a cup of tea and exchange of news. This would be followed by the serious business of trading at the unheated store. George Burnham describes the process.

> The trapper would pull the first white fox out of a sack and lay it across the counter. He would select some item, such as four pounds of tea, and Charlie [the manager] would indicate on the skin how much was used for the tea or how much was left. Another selection would be made and when goods had been purchased to the full value of the skin, Charlie would pull the skin over to our side of the counter and drop it onto the floor. Out would come another pelt and the trading was resumed. The fox skins were not put in the sack "willy nilly," no indeed, the best skin was always at the bottom and others laid on top so that the poorest skin was always the first to be traded. Thus, the trapper felt that the more he could squeeze on a poor skin, the more he would be able to get on the better skins. (Burnham 1986:105)

The Inuit trading into Walker Bay spent most of their time on the move, but Burnham reports that two Copper Inuit lived close by, full time, in a tent covered with moss and snowblocks. One of these was an old man, Nappayuak, who hobbled around on two canes and visited the HBC residence daily to warm himself at the stove. The other permanent resident, an Inuk

Fig. 4.9. Interior of Fort Collinson HBC post. Photo by Charles Rowan/ Courtesy of NWT Archives.

Fig. 4.10. Povotag and HBC clerk George Burnham standing at the base of the radio tower,
Fort Collinson, Walker Bay, 1935. Povotag
(right), a regular at the HBC trading post, was
only three feet tall, although in his twenties.
Holman elders say Povotag never grew to nor-
mal height because of a curse placed upon him
by a jealous stepmother when he was a boy.
Photo courtesy of George Burnham, Winnipeg.

named Povatag (Pogotak), was in his early 20s when Burnham
met him in 1935. He stood only 36 inches high and weighed 59
pounds. Burnham wrote of him:

> He was most intelligent and always "on the go." He owned his
> very own .22 calibre rifle and had cut down the stock for conve-
> nience in handling. He carried his own fine-cut tobacco and rolled
> his own cigarettes. They had one dog named Kavrak and the
> smallest sled I ever saw, it really was a one-dog sled, but they
> got around with it and maintained a small trap line (1986:107).

Even today, many Holman elders remember Povotag and agree that he was extremely smart and industrious. According to elder Ruth Nigiyonak, Povotag had been adopted as a child by a woman named Kuniluk, who for some reason had become jealous of him. She placed her hand on Povotag's head and said that he was never to grow tall. From that day on, Povotag remained small, even though he was prefectly capable of hunting, trapping, and caring for himself.

Getting supplies through to the trading posts at Walker Bay was often hampered by severe ice conditions in Amundsen Gulf. The HBC post usually received its yearly outfit via native schooners, such as the *Sea Otter*, which took on supplies at Tuktoyaktuk; but during the fall of 1934, for example, the *Sea Otter* was unable to make the crossing to Walker Bay. Supplies were ferried by dog-team from De Salis to Walker Bay. Difficulty in

Fig. 4.11. Povotag and Macara with bows and arrows, Fort Collinson, circa 1935. Photo by Charles Rowan, manager of the HBC post. Courtesy of NWT Archives.

resupplying is one reason why the HBC eventually (1939) decided to relocate its post back to Prince Albert Sound.

Missionaries and Mounties

In 1913, Fathers Rouviere and LeRoux, two Roman Catholic missionaries who had entered the region to find converts among the recently discovered Copper Inuit, were murdered by two Copper Inuit near what is now called Bloody Falls, on the Coppermine River (see R. G. Moyles 1979 for an interesting discussion of the arrest and trial of the two men, Uluksuk and Sinnisiak). This significantly slowed Roman Catholic missionary efforts in the region. The Anglican Church, too, was eager for converts among the Copper Inuit. In 1915, three Anglicans (Rev. H. Girling and assistants G. E. Merritt and W. H. B. Hoare) entered the region and by 1916 had established themselves at Bernard Harbor. This mission, relocated to Coppermine in 1928, was joined in 1929 by a Roman Catholic mission. The Anglicans, with a thirteen-year advantage over the Roman Catholics, had become firmly entrenched in the area and had gained converts (Usher 1965:57). Anglican missionaries (such as the Rev. J. Harold Webster, who replaced Girling) traveled widely from Coppermine to Prince Albert Sound and Cambridge Bay, gaining the loyalty of large numbers of Inuit families. Interviews with Holman elders Sam Oliktoak and Albert Palvik indicate that they had repeated contacts with Webster long before Roman Catholic missionaries became active in the area. Palvik reports that he and his wife along with two other couples were married by Webster on the ocean ice between Read Island and Bernard Harbor (probably in the early 1930s).

Six years after the 1913 Bloody Falls murders, the Northwest Mounted Police (later renamed the Royal Canadian Mounted Police) established a detachment at Tree River. It was later moved to Bernard Harbor to license traders entering the area. In 1932, it was moved again to Coppermine (Usher 1965:58). The people of Prince Albert Sound and Minto Inlet, because of their remote location, had minimal contact with the police during the 1920s. An early report (RCMP Coppermine Detachment, 1932) makes reference to a patrol of Prince Albert Sound around 1922, but indicates that was the only one until 1932. In the 1930s, the police initiated yearly patrols to all the trading posts and Inuit camps in Copper Eskimo territory, including Minto Inlet, Walker Bay, and Prince Albert Sound.

115

One of the first RCMP officers to make repeated visits to the trading posts and Inuit camps on Victoria Island was Corporal G. M. Wall. In February 1932, Wall left Coppermine with two guides and traveled to Rymer Point, Read Island, Prince Albert Sound, Minto Inlet, and Walker Bay. In his report, written upon his return to Coppermine, Wall made a number of interesting observations regarding the conditions of the Inuit groups he encountered. On islands off the north shore of Minto Inlet, Wall met a large group of Inuit and reported:

> This was the largest encampment visited in the country patrolled through, comprising 21 families. Some of the houses were joined together and others had passages leading off a main one to their own igloo. One native here had put up a 10 × 12 foot tent and built a snowhouse over it (RCMP Patrol Report 1932: 4).

There can be no doubt that this large encampment was inhabited by Copper Inuit, since the westerners who were beginning to enter the region did not build snowhouses, but tended to use tents or sod, blocked with snow. Wall's observations indicate that the large snowhouse settlements that had always been a feature of traditional Copper Inuit life were still in use even after traders had entered the region and encouraged people to take up trapping rather than seal hunting. Wall encountered the same group the following year, this time finding fourteen families camped on the ice in the middle of Minto Inlet (RCMP Patrol Report 1933:2).

Wall offers an interesting comparison between the Prince Albert Sound people and the Copper Inuit living around Read Island and Rymer Point:

> The natives on the southwest coat of Victoria Land had all done well trapping and in all the camps there was ample evidence of this. They were all well supplied with tea, sugar, biscuits, jam, etc. These natives are also getting away from the use of the seal oil lamps and although they had them they would use the primus lamps they had bought this winter, this may only be for a year as long as they can buy coal oil from the traders. The continual use of primus stoves does not tend towards cleanliness, and the houses are very dirty as was the clothing which had been purchased from the traders. The calico artigues [*sic*] and the men's trousers have been covered in grease and [are] dirty. . . . There was a remarkable difference in the Prince Albert Sound natives. These peoples did not have the white man's food and clothing,

[but were] depending on the country for food. The houses were all clean and tidy and they were all well clothed with deer skins, only using a very little white men's clothing. All the sleds, harpoons and equipment was all of the best and in good repair, also all the dogs were in fine condition. The people themselves were all a fine healthy looking bunch and there was only one case of sickness; this was a very old woman. These natives only go into Read Island once a [year] to trade, usually at the end of April and stay on the south coast of Victoria Land three or four weeks visiting the other relatives and then return again (RCMP Patrol Report 1933:7).

Wall's comments are echoed in later reports. By and large, those Copper Inuit who were in less direct contact with white traders seemed to be healthier and better clothed than those living closer to trading posts. Wall believed that the people of Minto Inlet ranked somewhere in between the people of Prince Albert Sound and the Inuit of southwest Victoria Island, possibly due to the influence of both the westerners and the two trading posts at Walker Bay.

Wall also reports that the drinking of denatured methyl hydrate was becoming common among all the Inuit groups visited in 1932, but that the "Prince Albert Sound natives only go in for this sort of thing when visiting the natives to the south." This is the first reference to this type of destructive behavior among the Inuit of western Victoria Island, and it is not surprising that drinking of methyl hydrate would start first among those natives in close proximity to the trading posts.

Wall also notes, during his 1932 tour, that missionaries (most likely Anglican) had already made progress in converting people to Christianity: "The influence of the missionaries is very noticeable and at all the camps visited the natives would show me their hymn books. The Minto Inlet natives held a service while I was there which consisted of singing six hymns. They observe Sunday very closely and will not do a thing, spending most of the day singing hymns even if the camp is out of meat" (RCMP Patrol Report 1933:7).

Another observation made by Wall during his 1932 patrol is fascinating. In assessing game conditions for the regions visited, Wall notes that caribou are very scarce, and that the people subsist primarily on seal, fish, and small game. To the north of Prince Albert Sound, he notes, "the natives hunt in the summertime and get a few caribou, but live chiefly on fish." Wall continues:

The Minto Inlet natives spend the summer around the post at Walker Bay and last summer they killed about 60 caribou roughly 20 miles north of the post. Apparently, there is a taboo on the northeast part of Victoria Land. The story is to the effect that a very long time ago, there were large herds of caribou and plenty of Eskimos in this part of the country. The different tribes fought battles amongst themselves and since then the natives will not go into this section of the country. This is all supposed to have happened when the present generation of men were small boys. It is quite possible that there may still be large herds of caribou there yet, as the country is well suited and wonderful feeding grounds (RCMP Patrol Report 1933:5).

Whatever the origin of this story, it did not prevent Andrew Klengenberg, George Avakana (Lena Klengenberg's husband), and William Kuptana (who was working as an interpreter for the Canalaska post) from setting up a temporary trapping camp at Deans Dundas Harbor the following year. They were able to kill a large number of caribou during the winter.

The RCMP reports of the early 1930s indicate that the Copper Inuit of Minto Inlet and Prince Albert Sound were still following a relatively traditional way of life. Some trapping was being carried out, but was usually abandoned after Christmas when people devoted all their time to seal hunting. Unlike the Copper Inuit around Rymer Point and Read Island, the Prince Albert Sound and Minto Inlet people were still relying on seal-oil lamps to heat and light their homes.

In 1937, a young Oblate missionary, Father Roger Buliard, left Coppermine for a reconnaissance of Victoria Island. His goal was to survey the country, take a census, make sketch maps of camp locations, and study the feasibility of establishing a mission among the people. He was accompanied by a young Inuk (whom he does not identify) and constable Chartrand (Wall's successor), who was going to Prince Albert Sound to investigate a rumor of murder. In Prince Albert Sound, the three travelers encountered a number of Inuit camps stretching the length of the sound.

Following Buliard's reconnaissance, it was decided to establish a small mission on the north shore of Prince Albert Sound and the Roman Catholic supply boat, *Our Lady of Lourdes*, sailed to Pitutok (Pitutuq), where building supplies and materials were unloaded. This small mission, located approximately ten miles east of the modern site of Holman, was to be only temporary providing Buliard with a base camp from which to explore further and decide the best location for a permanent mission. Although the new mission was created at the urging of Buliard, he was unable to accompany the supply boat and help with its construction: Buliard had been instructed to stay in Coppermine until December to help train the newly arrived Father Le Mer.

To build the temporary mission while he was occupied in Coppermine, Father Buliard recruited Tom (Konguak) Goose. Not only was Tom Goose a recent Catholic convert, but he had just been fired by the RCMP and was out of work. Goose agreed to go to Pitutok with his wife, Molly, to build the mission's base camp. By New Year's 1938, Goose returned to Coppermine by dog-team and informed Buliard that his new mission post was ready. Immediately (January 2), Buliard departed for Pitutok, accompanied by Tom and Molly Goose. Over the next few months, Buliard traveled throughout Prince Albert Sound, Minto Inlet, and even to Banks Island, seeking converts. He was able to convert some Inuit families, but met hostility in other cases, presumably from families that had already been converted by the Anglicans.

At the end of July, after his first winter of mission work, Buliard sailed to Tuktoyaktuk on an Inuit schooner in order to get supplies and make a report to his superior Bishop Fallaise. After receiving permission to continue his mission work on Victoria Island, Buliard moved his camp from Pitutok to Minto

Fig. 4.12. Photo taken during construction of new HBC post at King's Bay near Holman Island, fall 1939. Photo by A. L. Washburn. Courtesy of Hudson's Bay Company Archives, Provincial Archives of Manitoba, 1987/363-H-46/14, Neg. No. 7034.

Fig. 4.13. Temporary trapping camp at Ulukhaktok, fall 1933. Six years before the Hudson's Bay Company moved its post from Walker Bay to King's Bay, a group of western Inuit spent the winter trapping in the vicinity of Holman Island. This photograph shows three schooners (*Blue Fox, Shamrock,* and *Nanook*) along the shore of Queen's Bay near Ulukhaktok Bluff. The empty shoreline shown in this photograph is now the site of the modern community of Holman. Photo by Mrs. Peter Sidney. Courtesy of the National Archives of Canada, No. C38549, and of Peter Sidney and family.

to be in closer contact with the people. The new mission was located at the mouth of the Kuujuak River, a favorite camping spot for many Inuit families.

Buliard made frequent trips to all the camps in the area. Bishop Faillaise, wanted a permanent location for the mission and, after research, had decided that a protected bay near Holman Island was the most suitable. The bishop contacted the HBC, hoping that the Bay would also decide to relocate to the same site, to their mutual benefit. That spring (1939), a plane took Buliard out to Edmonton for a meeting. Accompanying him was a young Inuk (Nichol Uluariuk), who was being sent to Fort Smith for medical treatment and later to Aklavik for schooling (Nichol Uluariuk was the first person from either Minto or Prince Albert Sound to be sent out for schooling). The Canadian government had expressed a desire that all organizations be located at the same place, and Buliard met with HBC officials in Edmonton to decide on a location. The HBC decided that a return to Prince Albert Sound would be advantageous since that was the area where the vast majority of local Inuit were trapping. Many of the people who had moved to Minto Inlet in 1927 and 1928, when caribou were scarce, had moved back to Prince Albert Sound as the herds built back up. The Bay realized that a lot of Prince Albert Sound people were

120

Fig. 4.14. The *Blue Fox* at temporary trapping camp, Ulukhaktok, 1933/1934. Photo by Mrs. Peter Sidney. Courtesy of the National Archives of Canada, No. PA27677, and of Peter Sidney and family.

Fig. 4.15. Fox skins drying on line at Ulukhaktok trapping camp, 1934. Photo by Mrs. Peter Sidney. Courtesy of the National Archives of Canada, No. C38506, and of Peter Sidney and family.

trading at Read Island, not Fort Collinson, and that some of this trade was being sidetracked to the Bay's competitor, L. F. Semmler. By relocating to Prince Albert Sound, the Bay realized that it would capture the trade of the Prince Albert Sound people while retaining the trade of the Minto Inlet and Walker Bay people, who would have no other place to trade. Since the Canalaska Trading Company had been bought out by the Bay in 1938, resulting in a closing of the Walker Bay Canalaska post, the Bay had become the dominant trading company in Copper Inuit territory.

That summer, the HBC dismantled its store at Walker Bay and moved it to its new location near Holman Island. On August 16, 1939, the HBC schooner *Fort Ross* dropped anchor in a deep harbor near Ulukhaktok bluff, with supplies for constructing a permanent Roman Catholic mission. Father Buliard, given the privilege of naming the new settlement location, decided on "King's Bay." According to Buliard: "The name seemed appropriate for two reasons. First, because my new mission was to be dedicated to Christ the King, and second, because it seemed a fitting patriotic remembrance of a royal visit. His majesty King George VI had just been touring Canada—the first time a king had set foot in our country" (Buliard 1951:124).

Soon after the *Fort Ross's* arrival, a number of HBC officials arrived by plane and thus gave Buliard first choice of a building site. After a brief survey, Buliard picked a small plateau between the ocean and a small, freshwater lake—now named for him, Father's Lake. The HBC store located its buildings nearby, approximately 800 feet to the south, nestled between two small hills.[3]

The Bay and the R.C. mission were actually not the first arrivals to Ulukhaktok. In 1933, three Banks Island schooners, the *Blue Fox*, the *Shamrock*, and the *Nanuk*, had set up a temporary trapping camp on the shore of what was later named Queen's Bay. Some years later, around 1937, Natkusiak and his family moved to Ulukhaktok, becoming the first permanent residents of the King's Bay settlement (Agnes Nanogak, personal communication).

3. A year after the HBC and the Roman Catholic mission relocated to King's Bay, an RCMP schooner, the *St. Roch*, sailed into Walker Bay. It was forced to spend the winter (1940/1941) there. The *St. Roch*, under the command of Staff-Sergeant Henry Larsen, was on the first leg of its famous trip through the Northwest Passage, sailing both directions, which it did from west to east from 1940 to 1942 and from east to west in 1944. On its return voyage (Halifax to Vancouver) the *St. Roch* became the first ship to navigate the passage in a single season.

5. Growth of the Holman (Ulukhaktok) Settlement

The King's Bay Site, 1939 to 1966

DURING THE FIRST YEARS of the King's Bay settlement, only a handful of Inuit families were permanent residents. These included the families of Tommy Kongoak Goose, Natkusiak, Mark Emerak, and Jacob Nipalariuk (Nipalakyok). With the exception of Emerak, all of these families were from the west. Each family had different reasons for moving to the new post. Jacob Nipalariuk and his wife Agnes Nigiyok had been shipwrecked several years before in Prince Albert Sound and traveled to Holman in 1939 to help with construction of the Bay store. Natkusiak, who had moved his family to King's Bay several years before the HBC and the mission arrived, was getting old; he wanted a place where he could settle down for the remainder of his life. Natkusiak's adopted son, Jimmy Memogana, lived and traveled with Father Buliard during the early years of the settlement and since he had little gear of his own, he used that of Buliard and the mission in order to support himself and Natkusiak's family. For several years, Jimmy and Father Buliard operated a small store out of the Roman Catholic Mission, even competing to some extent with the neighboring HBC.

Ulukhaktok

Albert Palvik. When I first came to Ulukhaktok, there was nobody around. There was no settlement at all. We stayed mainly in

Fig. 5.1. *The Old Woman*, Holman Print Collection, 1980/81. Stonecut by Harry Egotak (artist and printer). Edition: 50. Courtesy of the Holman Eskimo Cooperative.

Minto Inlet and Prince Albert Sound. We passed through here, but it was not a place to stay. Later on, the Qablunaat came here and the people from the west [western Inuit from the Delta and Banks Island]. They built buildings at Ulukhaktok. People didn't usually camp right here. Mostly, they would go down around the islands and Iluvilik to hunt seal. I never heard about other people living here, even long ago. The only time I remember people moving here was when the trading post was built and the missionaries and westerners came here.

Elsie Nilgak. We always came here [Ulukhaktok] for Christmas and Easter as far back as I can remember. There weren't that many people living here then. The buildings that first came up here were the HBC building, the RC building, Nipilariuk's house, Kongoak's house, and Natkusiak's house. Those were the first people to be living here. After Nipilariuk died, I moved here. Long ago, those people used to live here. I only moved here

Fig. 5.2. Completed HBC complex at King's Bay, 1961. Photo by Villy Svarre. Courtesy of Hudson's Bay Company Archives, Provincial Archives of Manitoba, 1987/363-H-46/18, Neg. No. N7037.

after there were quite a few people living here. Those people from Qiqiqtanayuk [Read Island] were living here too. Allen Joss and his family and the Kuneyunas came here by dog-team in spring before the ice break-up [June 1962]. Then, after the ice was gone, Billy Joss and Ekootaks came up here on Billy Joss's boat [the *Kingalik*]. And the George Okheenas came up on Jorgen's [Klengenberg's] boat [the *Polar Bear*]. Those people were among the very last people to come up from that side of Prince Albert Sound.

All those people who first moved to Holman built their own houses with tents and plywood. Through the winter, they would put snow on the outside walls to make it warm. That's how they started to make the first houses. They also used seal oil rather than fuel oil to keep warm. Back then, all of us used only kudliqs inside the house, like the kudliqs our grandparents and great-grandparents used long ago.

Modern conveniences came very slowly to the small, isolated outpost. According to Buliard's book on the early years of what was then called the King's Bay Mission, a wind generator was set up for the mission in 1941 to provide electricity for the mission buildings. Two years later, the mission obtained a motorized fishing boat from Vancouver, the *Mary*, which was used for hunting, fishing, and visiting Inuit camps in Prince Albert Sound and Minto Inlet.

While there were few caribou or musk ox near the new post, the Holman area provided an abundance of seals, fish, and small game. For caribou, it was necessary to travel across Minto Inlet by dog-team, a round-trip that took considerably longer than it does now by snowmobile.

Building with Ice

Elsie Nilgak. We had no [wood] house when we lived at Pitutak before we moved to Holman. When the winter season was coming, I'd put up my tent by the ocean shore. And when the bay

Fig. 5.3. Roman Catholic Mission building at King's Bay (Holman), 1954, showing at left the wind generator. Soon after the construction of the new mission building at King's Bay, Father Buliard installed a wind generator to provide electricity to the mission. Photo by James Watt Anderson. Courtesy of Hudson's Bay Company Archives, Provincial Archives of Manitoba, 1986/45-1048, Neg. No. N7078.

126

Fig. 5.4. The *Mary*, near King's Bay, showing the boat's new deck and cabin. Photo by Father Maurice Metayer. Courtesy of the Holman Community Education Council.

would freeze up, then I would build a house out on the ice and put my tent up inside. Then that's where we would spend the winter season. We built walls first with ice and then put the tent up inside and then used caribou skins to cover the top. All the skins that are put together. We used it like a lid for the ice walls. Those houses were warm in the winter. That's how I was taught. It wasn't like I didn't know how. I was taught by my parents and grandparents. Those were people before me.

Most of the Copper Inuit families in Minto Inlet and Prince Albert Sound continued a relatively traditional way of life, but one that was becoming increasingly oriented to fox trapping. A number of Prince Albert Sound people continued to trade at Read Island, but most of the regional population started trading into Holman. By 1939, the number of trading posts in the Holman-Coppermine region had declined dramatically as the Hudson's Bay Company came to dominate the trade and put competitors out of business. Ikey Bolt's trading post at Rymer Point closed down around 1937; Lena Klengenberg and George Avakana's post at Cape Krusenstern was closed down in 1936 (Usher 1965:54–55).

As the Inuit of the Holman region developed a taste for trade items such as tea, sugar, tobacco, and flour, they began to rely more heavily on fur trapping as a means to purchase these items. The transition from traditional ways was undoubtedly assisted by the Copper Inuit's contact with the western Inuit (or Walliningmiut), who had developed a reputation for being superb trappers. Increased dependence upon trapping, however, changed the Inuit economy. Since trappers had to tend their traplines during the winter, they had less time to devote to midwinter subsistence activities such as sealing, caribou hunting, and polar bear hunting. The more involved people became in trapping, the more dependent they became upon goods purchased at the trading posts. Moreover, the size of dog-teams increased. In the early part of the century, anthropologist Diamond Jenness had noted that the typical Copper Inuit family rarely owned more than two or three dogs (Jenness 1922:118). Trapping, however, required greater mobility and hence a larger number of dogs per active trapper. Inuit families trapping for the fur trade had a larger number of dogs to care for and feed. Fortunately for them, the introduction of rifles and fishnets helped to increase their efficiency and trapper families were able to feed both themselves and their dogs.

Trading at Holman

Elsie Nilgak. There were no lights in that HBC store. When it was time to trade and shop, that's when they would put the stove and the fuel-oil lanterns on. And when Christmas was nearing, the stove and the lanterns were always on, keeping the place warm and welcoming the people for Christmas. People also came at Easter time. When people came at Christmas and Easter, that's when there would be lots of snowhouses along King's Bay. And they would have drum-dances at Father's house [the RC Mission] or in one of the HBC warehouses. The westerners and Prince Albert Sound people also used to have square dances. They used to have lots of dances when I was young.

Agnes Goose. I remember as an adult that people from Prince Albert Sound and Minto would come here for Easter and Christmas. They would come here and would build lots of snowhouses. They would have dog races, dances, and play games. That was lots of fun.

Fig. 5.5. Minto Inlet camp at the north of the Kuujjuak River. From front to back: Morris Nigiyok, Frank Kudlak, Philip Haogak, Harry Egotak, Roy Inuktalik, and Esau Ilgayak. Photo by Father Maurice Metayer. Courtesy of the Holman Community Education Council.

This process of economic change occurred at different rates for the Holman and Coppermine regions. The Copper Inuit around Coppermine and Read Island made the transition much earlier than the people of Prince Albert Sound. By the 1940s, however, trapping was firmly entrenched in the Holman region.

Although the trading posts provided Inuit trappers with valued goods which presumably made their lives easier, the relationship between trapper and trader was not always to the benefit of the trapper. As Peter Usher (1965:62) notes:

> The relationship of the Eskimo to the trader became virtually that of a bonded servant. To trap initially the Eskimo had to be supplied with traps, and generally a rifle and other gear. Having no means to pay for this outfit, he went in "debt" to the trader, and settled his account the following spring by bringing in his catch of furs. Both the availability of the white fox and its market price fluctuated considerably, and in some years the Eskimo was unable to pay his debts. This indebtedness prevailed for almost thirty years, until other sources of cash became available to the Eskimos.

Fig. 5.6. John Kaodloak and Susie Tiktalik. Photo by Father Maurice Metayer. Courtesy of the Holman Community Education Council.

In the Holman region, these "other sources" came in the late 1950s and early 1960s, in the form of a developing arts and crafts industry, government employment, family allowances, and social assistance, all of which helped increase the size and importance of the Holman settlement. In the Coppermine and Read Island areas, many Inuit obtained employment at DEW (Distant Early Warning) line-sites, the construction of which commenced in 1955. Since the Holman region was far removed from the major DEW line-sites, such employment (as well as the negative consequences of such employment) had minimal impact.

The productivity of trapping as an economic pursuit varied not only from one year to the next but also by region. The RCMP Annual Reports of 1952 noted:

> At Prince Albert Sound, only two families dwell there even though this area has been reputed for its good fishing, caribou hunting, and presence of fur-bearing animals for quite some time. One of the reasons why more natives do not reside in this area appears to be fear of Eskimo Fred Kahak, who attempts to claim such

area as his domain. . . . The two families at that point, both Kahak and Pogotak, each had good quantities of fish and caribou as well as seal . . . [obtained] between visits to their traplines. It was established that more foxes had been caught by these two individual families at that time than any other trapper [trading into the] Read Island or Holman Island posts. Caribou had migrated in a small herd fairly close to their camps during the late fall of 1952. . . . These two families were short of nothing for themselves and their dogs. (RCMP Annual Report, Coppermine Detachment 1952:2)

During the same year, however, the fourteen families in Minto Inlet (scattered among five different camps) were experiencing an extremely poor trapping year. In fact, the people in Minto Inlet complained to the RCMP that they were unable to get credit at the Bay:

The natives in that area complained to the writer that they could not obtain debt [credit] in order to purchase their necessities from the Hudson's Bay Company trading post at Holman Island. This matter was taken up with Mr. Hall, the local post manager at that point, and his attention was drawn to the responsibility of such company to issue relief or debt to all able-bodied trappers and hunters during these poor fur years to prevent undue hardship, and not through the medium of Government Destitute Relief or over-issues of certain articles on Family Allowance. Mr. Hall assured the writer he would issue relief through his department as circumstances warranted (RCMP Annual Report, Coppermine Detachment 1952:2)[1]

From 1940 to the early 1960s, the permanent Inuit population of Holman fluctuated between four and seven families. Throughout this period, the greatest concentration of people was in Minto Inlet and Prince Albert Sound. Almost all of these families traded at the Holman HBC post, although a few Prince Albert Sound families continued trading at Read Island until its closure in 1962. For Holman, the major ingathering periods of the year were Christmas, Easter and the fall, around the time of the arrival of the barge. These were often quite festive occasions as large numbers of families came together to trade,

1. In many areas of northern Canada, where there was no RCMP detachment, the manager of the local Hudson's Bay Company store was often responsible for issuing relief payments to the needy.

socialize, dance, and play games. Many of the families living in camps out on the land continued to live in snowhouses in winter and in canvas or skin tents (often with a wood frame) in summer. By the late 1950s, a number of camps in Prince Albert Sound and Minto had permanent dwellings, constructed of scrap lumber, canvas, and other materials. Matthew Malgokak, for example, built a permanent dwelling at Berkeley Point and eventually installed a wind generator, obtained from the Roman Catholic Mission. All of these buildings were eventually abandoned as people moved from the camps into Holman.

Fig. 5.7. Joseph Kitekudlak and Matthew Malgokak at King's Bay (Holman), 1952. For many years, Malgogak and his family lived at a permanent trapping camp at Berkeley Point. After his death in 1967, the family moved to Holman. Photo by Father Maurice Metayer. Courtesy of the Holman Community Education Council.

Fig. 5.8. Roy Inuktalik and Joseph Kitekudlak on whaleboat at Minto. The owner of the boat, Matthew Malgogak, was one of the first trappers in the Holman region to purchase a whaleboat with an inboard motor. Photo by Father Maurice Metayer. Courtesy of the Holman Community Education Council.

The Roman Catholic Mission

In September 1949, Father Henri Tardy arrived in Holman to assist Father Buliard at the Roman Catholic Mission. Several months later, when Buliard accidentally shot himself while setting his rifle and had to be evacuated on the HBC's plane (March 19, 1950), Tardy was left with responsibility for the mission. Father Buliard recovered but did not return to Holman.

As in most of the missions in the North at the time, both Catholic and Anglican, much time was spent in everyday chores and maintenance activities, including hunting, feeding the dogs, cutting ice, fetching water, preparing food, and so on. Father Maurice Metayer was a frequent visitor to the Holman mission and with his assistance and advice Tardy continued Buliard's work. The mission operated a small fishing boat, the *Mary*, which was used for traveling and hunting. In the summer of 1953 or 1954, Tardy, Metayer, Alec (Aliknak) Banksland, and Jimmy Memogana built a deck and small deckhouse on the

Fig. 5.9. Father Henri Tardy on the Roman Catholic Mission craft
Mary, before decking was built on the boat. Photo by Father Maurice
Metayer. Courtesy of the Holman Community Education Council.

Mary, making it a more comfortable boat for long trips. Another
project started in 1957, when Tardy, assisted by Jack Goose,
Jimmy Memorana, and Nicholas Uluariuk, built a small mission outpost at the mouth of the Kuujjuak River, to be used in
summer for hunting seals and visiting the families of that region. The mission in Holman did not have a large following,
since most people had been converted early to the Anglican
faith. It was, nevertheless, a major gathering place for people
arriving to the settlement to trade and socialize. During ingath-
erings, the R.C. mission was filled with people playing games
and conversing over endless cups of tea.

The Anglican Church in Holman

Although Anglican missionaries had been successful in converting many Holman area residents before the arrival of Buli-

ard, they were slow to establish a permanent mission in the community. A small Anglican church was built by local residents under the direction of Anglican catechist Sam Oliktoak in 1962, and in 1963 a full-time Anglican minister named Robert Beresford (Bery) Capron, arrived in the community.[2] Prior to this, Holman residents organized their own Anglican services and received an annual visit from the minister in Coppermine. Capron arrived March 21, 1963, on the first of a series of airlifts ferrying supplies to Holman for the construction of a mission residence. The house was built that spring and summer by Capron and his congregation. In August, Capron was joined by his fiancée, Drina Staines, and within an hour or so of her arrival the two were married by Archdeacon J. R. Sperry from Coppermine. Drina Capron helped organize the Anglican Sunday school and, as a registered nurse, provided medical care. Bery Capron meanwhile had to make annual visits to Sach's Harbor, which at the time was an outpost of the Holman Anglican Mission. These visits were usually done in spring, by dog-team.

The Roman Catholic mission made intense efforts to retain its influential position, but the Anglican faith eventually prevailed, attracting the majority of Holman residents. At times, the competition between Anglican and Catholic missionaries showed signs of conflict. The goal of both groups was, of course, to gain converts to their particular faith, and it was not uncommon for there to be mutual suspicion between the two groups. From 1939 to 1963, such problems were minimal since the Anglicans did not have a full-time missionary present. With Capron's arrival, however, tensions rose. Tempers occasionally flared, notably in a few cases involving "mixed" marriages. It was apparent to Capron that the Roman Catholic Mission intended to bar no expense in its attempt to win over converts and he wrote in the first *Annual Report of the Church of the Resurrection,* in December 1963:

Opposition from the Romans has been considerable. This is hardly to be wondered at. They have ruled supreme for many years and to have to face opposition is something new to them. Prior to this year, this station has been visited annually as an outpost of Coppermine. Outwardly, the Romans have been very friendly and helpful. However, there have been two lay brothers here throughout the summer and they have been engaged in a

2. Between June 1958 and February 1959, Sam Oliktoak completed catechist studies in Coppermine under the Reverend John Sperry.

large building programme of their own. They have built two
large halls. One is being used as a church and residence for the
Roman Priest [Father Tardy] and also a reading room and visiting room for the people. The other is a classroom for the "pre-
schoolers" and also a large recreation room for the people. In
this room, they have dances and parties and movie shows. They
also have provided a pool table and a tennis table and darts
and various other games. The recreation room must measure
approximately 40' × 24'. In August [1963], two sisters arrived
and these have been engaged in teaching school for those who
want to go. Two classes are held—one is for those who have never
been to school before, and the other is for those who have.

The Roman Catholic Mission was clearly able to outspend the
Anglicans in both buildings and manpower. Anglican resources
were minimal compared with the Roman Catholics. Correspondence from Capron to his superior, Bishop Donald Marsh, in
Toronto, indicates that the Holman Anglican Mission operated
on a meager budget, barely able to obtain sufficient funding
for heating-oil and Sunday school supplies. While the Roman
Catholics brought in "carpenter brothers" to construct buildings, the Anglicans had to rely on volunteer labor from parish-
ioners.[3] This disparity may have been another factor contributing to tension between the two missions.

Another area of conflict pertained to the allocation of lots for
the new settlement site on Queen's Bay. Lots were allocated
while Capron was out of the community on business and when
he returned he learned that the Roman Catholics had been
given spaces in the center of the new town site. The Anglican
lots were to be some distance from the town center. This was
viewed by Capron as a major setback. He had hoped to obtain
the block of lots that was secured by the Roman Catholic
Mission.

Capron departed Holman in May 1965, and was replaced the
following February by Nigel Wilford, who oversaw the move
of buildings from the King's Bay site to the new site on Queen's
Bay.[4] Even though the new Anglican location was at the edge

3. The Anglican and Catholic building projects suggest a fundamental
difference in approach to the issue of community involvement between the
two faiths. The Roman Catholics brought in carpenters and the buildings
ostensibly were given to the community; the Anglicans relied on their members and quite probably this resulted in a greater sense of ownership (and
perhaps pride).

4. Anglican ministers for the Holman community were: Robert Beresford
Capron (March 1943 to May 1965); Nigel Wilford (February 1966 to July

of town, it was not long before the community expanded, to surround the new Anglican Mission complex.

Health and Disease

Before the arrival of Eurocanadians to the Canadian Arctic, the Inuit were a relatively healthy people. Deaths due to hunting accidents and starvation were common (and life expectancy was relatively short), but the Inuit were free of major infectious disease. According to anthropologist Diamond Jenness, in 1914 disease was virtually unknown between Coronation Gulf and the magnetic pole (1964:140). In ensuing decades, following increased contact with white traders, missionaries, and police, the Copper Inuit fell prey to tuberculosis, influenza, measles, and venereal disease. Many of these diseases proved fatal to the Inuit, who had no natural immunity.

As early as 1927 and 1928, an influenza epidemic killed half the Inuit population of Bernard Harbour. The onset of this epidemic coincided with the arrival of the HBC supply ship *Baychimo*, which also brought the Reverend J. Harold Webster, who converted many of the Inuit of the Holman-Coppermine region to the Anglican faith. Other fatal epidemics occurred throughout the 1930s, 1940s, and 1950s. Tuberculosis, especially, was a chronic health problem from the early 1930s until the 1970s.

Recognizing the poor health conditions of the Copper Inuit, the government appointed Russell Martin to be the resident doctor at Coppermine. As the only doctor between Aklavik and Chesterfield Inlet, Dr. Martin was responsible for a population scattered over a one-thousand-mile stretch of arctic coast. Given inadequate funding, Martin was unable to combat the many illnesses that were beginning to plague the Inuit. Two years after his appointment, he went to Ottawa to plead for increased funding but Canada, in the midst of the economic depression in the early 1930s, was unwilling to spend more

---

1966); Terry Buckle (August 1966 to June 1970); Geoffrey Dixon (July 1976 to May 1978); Larry Robertson (January 1980 to February 1981); R. Haydn Schofield (April 1984 to May 1988); Tim Chesterton (August 1988 to July 1991). The Holman Anglicans also always had strong lay leadership: catechists Sam Oliktoak and Morris Nigiyok, and lay readers Jimmy Kudlak, Essau Elgayak, and Robert Kuptana. There is also an active women's auxillary (Angnait Ekayuktaukatigiit), which meets on a regular basis.

money on medical facilities for the North. In fact, the government decided to close the medical station in Coppermine, and Dr. Martin never returned (Finnie 1940:167–168).

After Martin's departure, medical treatment was provided by Webster, the Anglican missionary. Finally, in 1948, a permanent nursing station was established, the same year that a school was built in Coppermine (Usher 1965:114). In Holman, medical treatment was sporadically provided by missionaries (primarily Father Tardy, Father Metayer, and Drina Capron), HBC managers, and RCMPs. After the Coppermine nursing station was opened, the resident nurse made periodic visits to Holman to provide medical care. Holman received its own nursing station in 1972.

From the 1930s, tuberculosis was one of the major illnesses affecting all of the Inuit, throughout the Canadian Arctic. Systematic tuberculosis X-ray surveys, however, did not begin in the Holman-Coppermine region until the spring of 1953. After 1953, these surveys, carried out by plane throughout the Kitikmeot region, were an annual event, taking advantage of the usually good spring traveling conditions and the, by then, deeply ingrained habit of the Inuit to gather for a couple of weeks around the missions and trading posts at Easter (Dr. Otto Schaefer, personal communication). Patients found to have advanced tubercular infections were flown out immediately to TB sanatoria, first in Aklavik, and later to Sir Charles Camsell Hospital in Edmonton.

These evacuations, although necessary, often proved to be very stressful and disruptive to Inuit families, who might find themselves without a mother or a father for years on end. The duration of TB treatment could vary, from several months to several years, depending upon the severity of the infection. One man from Holman was forced to spend almost ten years in Edmonton separated from family and friends. By and large, however, the Inuit from the Holman region were not as dramatically affected by TB as Inuit in the Coppermine region. Between 1962 and 1966, only 4.2 percent of the people from the Holman region were evacuated for TB; this is to be compared with 11.3 percent for the Coppermine region. Dr. Otto Schaefer (personal communication) believes that this lower rate for Holman families was due to a better and more traditional diet, compared with the Coppermine Inuit, who relied more heavily on southern foods from the HBC store.

These diseases, plus a high infant-mortality rate, had a significant impact upon the numbers of Copper Inuit. Usher

(1965:67) believes that the Inuit population of the Holman-Coppermine region remained relatively stable between 1914 and 1924. Thereafter, evidence suggests the population declined sharply. Usher writes: "Most likely the actual nadir in population came in the early 1930s, from which a recovery was already being made by 1942. Indications are that a full return to the pre-contact population level was not made until the mid-1950s" (1965:68–69).

In the late 1950s and the 1960s, the Holman-Coppermine region experienced a dramatic population explosion. This expansion was due to the government's TB eradication program, better medical treatment (especially prenatal and post-natal health care), and the introduction of bottle-feeding.[5] Similar population increases occurred in Inuit communities throughout the Canadian Arctic.

The Holman Settlement in 1963

In the summer of 1963, an economic survey was conducted in the Holman-Coppermine region by the Department of Northern Affairs and National Resources (Usher 1965). The results of this area survey provide a useful description of the Holman community twenty-four years after its founding and three years prior to its relocation to Queen's Bay, its present site.

In 1963, Holman was still on the east shore of King's Bay—the original 1939 location. By this time, the vast majority of Inuit in the Holman trading area had taken up permanent residence in the community. This movement, consolidating the community, took place extremely rapidly and was largely due to the government's decision to build seven prefabricated, matchbox (Plan 370) units at the King's Bay site. According to one Holman elder (Elsie Nilgak), many people from Prince Albert Sound and Minto Inlet moved to Holman in 1962 and 1963, hoping to get a government house. The first houses were

---

5. Traditionally, Inuit children were breast-fed for three to five years and sometimes into the sixth and seventh years. Prolonged breast-feeding was practiced by many precontact hunting and gathering populations to ensure the survival of offspring. Recent research has shown that prolonged breast-feeding inhibits ovulation, making for longer intervals between children. With the introduction to the Arctic of bottle-feeding in the late 1950s and early 1960s, the traditional strategy of birth control and birth spacing was disrupted. This, in turn, led to an increase in live births, resulting in a significant shortening of birth intervals.

Fig. 5.10. King's Bay settlement site before the move to Queen's Bay. Photo by Father Henri Tardy. Courtesy of the Holman Community Education Council.

allocated to the families of widows, elderly persons, and unmarried women with children. In the mid- to late 1960s, as more government housing became available, houses were allocated to all types of families.

First Houses in Holman

Elsie Nilgak. The first houses [public housing] that were built here were those box houses back around 1962–1963. They were first built across [on King's Bay] for the iliagyuit—those of us who either had a large family or had no parents [these houses were also called welfare houses]. We were known as iliagyuit—families like myself with Kalvak, Patsy, Mark, Alice, and Winnie—also Ailanak and her kids, and Kitulgitak, Ida, and Adam. We, the iliagyuit, were the first ones to get houses. That following summer, more matchbox houses were built for people. That's when a lot of people started to move into town from Minto and Prince Albert Sound.

When I started living in a matchbox, I had a fuel-oil stove, but we ran out of fuel oil rather quick. And those houses weren't all that warm. My big kudliq used seal-fat oil. I put something under it for a platform and used it in the house. I used the platform to prevent the floor from getting dirty. That's how those

140

first people who were here used to live back then using those kudliqs. And when and if they wanted the seal-oil stove on, that's when they would put them on. And the rest of the times when the stove wasn't on, they would use the kudliqs. That's how we used to live.

Those box houses had lots of people in them, but there was enough room for all of us and the kids. That's where we spent the winter. When I got my box house, it seemed so big—lots of room.

By the summer of 1963, Holman's population was 115, with twelve people continuing to reside in Minto (at Kuujjuak) and eight people at Berkeley Point. Following the Read Island HBC post closure (July 1962), Holman also included a number of families (Kuneyuna, Joss, Okheena) recently relocated to Holman. The settlement consisted of the Roman Catholic Mission, the HBC, the Anglican Mission with its residence (both recently constructed), eight frame houses (seven of which were low-cost government structures built the year before), and ten scrap houses. The prefabricated houses were all one-room houses, each with only 288 square feet of floor space, but equipped with a small bathroom, oil stove, water tank, and sink. None of these units, however, had bathtubs or electrical wiring. By comparison, conditions in the scrap houses were extremely poor. While all the low-cost government houses were equipped with bag-and-pail honey-buckets, none of the scrap houses had interior toilets. Residents of the scrap houses had to go outside in summer or to use a tin can (or some other form of chamber pot) in winter. In summer, anyway, until mid-September, people usually moved out of their houses and into tents.

In the absence of municipal water and sanitation services, people had to fetch their own water and dispose of their own garbage and sewage. In summer, water was hauled in pails from Father's Lake; in winter, large blocks of ice were cut and hauled to houses by dog-team. The disposal of sewage was less satisfactory. In winter, it was dumped out on the ice of King's Bay; in summer it was emptied directly into the bay. In the early 1960s, plastic bags were not provided with the honey-buckets and people spilled sewage directly out of the toilet pail. Garbage was burned or dumped into open pits close to the houses. Only one Inuit house was equipped with electricity (most likely the house of Tommy Goose). In general, housing conditions during this early period were quite poor and must

Fig. 5.11. Father Maurice Metayer, Bill Joss, and Allen Joss at Read
Island. In 1931, the HBC opened a post at Read Island, off the southwestern coast of Victoria Island. Between 1929 and 1962, five different
trading posts were established on Read Island, including the HBC,
Canalaska Trading Company, Craig and Daigle, L. F. Semmler, and
Johnny Norberg. The HBC eventually dominated the others (as it did
throughout the Canadian Arctic). In 1962, the HBC post at Read Island
was closed, and its store relocated to King's Bay (Holman)—the manager, Bill Joss, being transfered to Holman. Not only did Joss bring
along his own Inuit family, he was also accompanied by other Read
Islanders. The closing of the Read Island store had a significant impact
on Inuit populations. Those who had traded at Read Island moved
to either Holman or Coppermine. Those who lived deep in Prince
Albert Sound redirected their trade to Holman. Photo by Father Maurice Metayer. Courtesy of the Holman Community Education Council.

have been a factor in the population's poor health, especially
with regard to TB infection.

Although all of the government houses were equipped with
fuel-oil cooking stoves, the high cost of heating-oil made the
use of these stoves much too expensive for most residents. Usher
(1965:108) notes that while heating-oil cost only 17.3 cents a
gallon in Montreal (in 1963), it cost 79 cents a gallon in the
North. Many people in Holman continued to rely on seal oil
as the primary source of home heating, burning it in either
traditional soapstone lamps, homemade stoves, or southern
cooking stoves.

Fig. 5.12. Agnes Goose (Nanogak) and Billy
Goose carrying fresh ice from Father's Lake,
early 1950s. Up until the late 1960s, Holman
residents were responsible for hauling their
own water or ice and disposing of their own
garbage and sewage. Once the community was
relocated to the Queen's Bay site, municipal
services (water delivery and garbage pickup)
were finally provided to all households. Photo
by Father Maurice Metayer. Courtesy of the
Holman Community Education Council.

A federal day school had not yet been built in Holman and
students had to be sent out to Inuvik for schooling. Although
a few Holman youngsters had been sent out to the Anglican
and Roman Catholic boarding schools in Aklavik since the late
1930s and early 1940s, it was not until the construction of the
federal boarding school in Inuvik that Holman students were
sent out in great numbers. In 1962, thirteen out of forty-two
Holman youngsters were attending school in Inuvik (Usher

Fig. 5.13. Simon Kataoyak and Billy Goose sawing ice blocks from
Father's Lake, early 1950s. All members of the family helped to cut
and haul the ice that was used for fresh drinking water throughout
the winter. These ice blocks would be piled outside of residences
and chipped away at when water was required. Even though water
delivery services were instituted in the late 1960s, Holman residents
continued to cut and haul ice to be used for tea and coffee. Even
today, most residents agree that water from lake ice tastes superior
to water that is delivered by truck. Photo by Father Maurice Metayer.
Courtesy of the Holman Community Education Council.

1965:119). In October 1963, the Roman Catholic Mission opened
a kindergarten, which met afternoons in the mission's recently
built Quonset hut—a hut that later became the craft shop for
the Holman Eskimo Cooperative (Monique Piche, personal communication). Between eight and fifteen children, aged from four
to eleven, attended regularly. Older children often accompanied
younger brothers and sisters to help watch over them. This day
school operated for three years, but closed with the opening of
a federal day school in the spring of 1966. During the last winter
of the kindergarten's operation, part of the community had
already been moved to the new settlement site along Queen's
Bay. As a result, the lay missionary who operated the school,

Monique Piche, drove the children to and from school on a sled pulled by a Ski-Doo.

In 1963, transportation into Holman was limited to the yearly barge operated by Northern Transportation Company or by chartered airplane. No airline had regularly scheduled flights to or from the community. Charters usually landed on King's Bay, using skis or wheels in winter or using floats in summer. King's Bay was the primary landing site, the community was essentially cut off from the outside world during freeze-up and break-up. Occasionally, however, planes with low-pressure tires were able to land on the raised beach of Queen's Bay.

The economy of Holman in the early 1960s was still heavily dependent upon trapping, sealing, and subsistence hunting. In 1962, the price of sealskin increased dramatically, providing another important source of income for Inuit hunters, not just in Holman but throughout the North. Records of fur trading indicate that in 1961/1962, 362 sealskins were traded at Hol-

Fig. 5.14. Refueling plane on King's Bay, early 1950s. Up until the late 1960s, plane flights into Holman were irregular. No scheduled flights serviced the community, only planes chartered by the Hudson's Bay Company, the missions and the government. A weekly scheduled flight was finally instituted in the early 1970s. Photo by Father Maurice Metayer. Courtesy of the Holman Community Education Council.

man. This figure jumped to 1,726 in 1962/1963 (Usher 1965:168). Not only did seal hunting provide much needed income for the Holman area, but the seal meat was used to feed dog-teams. At the time, Holman area hunters maintained twenty-seven dog teams (a total of 259 dogs) but not a single snowmobile. Seals were hunted using three major techniques: seal hooks in winter, seal stalking in spring, and open-water hunting by boat in summer.

Polar Bear Hunting

Morris Nigiyok. When I was fourteen years old, I was trapping alone around Minto. At that time, prices were really good. Maybe between thirty and forty dollars. Really good trapping too. Lots of foxes. At that time, I shot my first polar bear—with my brother-in-law Philip Haogak. He asked me to go with him. He told me he's going to hunt polar bear. He asked me: "You want to come along?" I said, "Yes." We went down to Nelson Head. We saw three polar bear. We got all of them, but we got no more gas. We stayed down there even though we don't have any gas. Always have tea. Always have good meat to eat. You know, old people know what to do. Not like today. Even with no gas, they don't care. Always have dry clothes, dry boots and mitts, everything. Only no gas. [When we got back], I sold my bearskin to the Bay. You know how much? It was about a nine-foot bear. I got twenty-five dollars for it. Twenty-five dollars was lots of money back then. Pilot biscuits at the time were seventy-five cents. Now, it's three dollars. Butter was ninety cents. Thirty-thirty ammunition was two dollars per box. Twenty-two short was forty-five cents a box. Gas was fifty cents a gallon.

Since the number of caribou in the Holman region in the early 1960s was very low, seals provided one of the more important sources of meat, for humans and dogs alike. Holman area hunters generally had to cross to Banks Island or to the north shore of Minto Inlet to hunt caribou. Usher (1965:174) estimates that in 1963 the people of the Holman area shot only about 150 to 200 caribou.

Fish constituted an important part of the Holman diet in those days, as it does today. By 1963, the fall trek to Fish Lake had become an important event in the seasonal subsistence cycle. Hunters travelled to Fish Lake in mid-October by dog-team to set nets under the ice. Fishnets were also set in the ocean during the summer around Holman and near the mouth of the Kuujjuak River at Minto.

The price of fox furs was lower than in previous decades, but trapping continued to be an important source of income. The sale of fox furs and sealskin provided approximately 45 percent of income for families living at Holman and adjacent camps. In 1962/1963, the average fur income of Holman families was $842 per family (Usher 1965:204). The remainder of cash income came from handicrafts production (approximately 10 percent), social security (approximately 15 percent), relief payments (approximately 25 percent), and casual employment for wages (approximately 5 percent). Unlike Coppermine, where almost 25 percent of income was derived from permanent wage labor, Holman had extremely few wage jobs in the early 1960s. Because of the low level of personal cash income in Holman ($1,850 per family for the region), the consumption of local foods far outweighed the consumption of store-bought foods (Usher 1965:219).

Although, in the early 1960s, snowmobiles had not yet been introduced into the Holman region, most families did own either a jolly boat or a freight canoe. Usher (1965:235) notes that the Holman Inuit had a total of twenty three-boats and twenty-one outboard motors. The most common outboard motors were 5.5 and 10 horsepower engines. By this time, most of the Inuit-owned schooners that had been used by the western Inuit to travel to and from Banks and Victoria Island in the 1930s and 1940s had fallen into disrepair and were no longer used. Prior to the introduction of outboard motors, Inuit who owned canoes or jolly boats relied upon either wind or their own muscle power to propel the crafts. According to one Holman elder, Nicholas Uluariuk, it would usually take two days to travel from Holman to the mouth of the Kuujjuak River, a trip that can be accomplished today, in three or four hours. A few people (for example, Albert Palvik and Matthew Malgokak) were able to purchase either jolly boats or whaleboats with inboard, air-cooled engines. According to Father Tardy, the first outboard motor was purchased by Father Buliard, in 1948. Soon afterward, others in the Holman region started to purchase these motors as well.

Motorboats

Agnes Goose. We always used to make boat trips by rowing. So when we first got kickers, it seemed really noisy and smelly. We

used to be able to taste it in the food. Like in the fish and seal—
from the smoke of the kicker. I couldn't stand the smell, but
nowadays, it doesn't seem to bother anyone. I remember traveling in a boat like this [with no motor]. We used to travel around
here. There were lots of seals close to town in those days before
we got kickers.

In 1963, the HBC was still the only retail outlet in the community. Prices at the Bay were, of course, considerably lower than
they are today, but it may be of interest to list some of them.
Usher (1965:272–273) notes the prices of some items at the
Holman HBC store during his summer visit in 1963. These are
compared to prices collected in the summer of 1991:

Item	1963 $CAN	1991 $CAN
butter (1 lb. can)	1.05	3.84
evaporated milk (one 12 fluid oz. can)	.25	1.57
tea (1 lb. package)	1.45	4.89
coffee (1 lb. can)	.95	4.32
chocolate bar	.13	.91
soft drinks	.30	1.41
cigarettes (20)	.40	7.50
gas (1 gall. leaded)	1.20	3.40
222 shells (20)	3.60	18.98
222 rifle	69.95	649.00
20 ft. canoe	500.00	NA
10 hp outboard motor	450.00	3,200.00
traps(size 1½)	.95	3.79

It is interesting to note that as early as 1962 and 1963, soda
pop and candy bars were frequently purchased at the store.

The Holman Eskimo Cooperative

The Holman Eskimo Cooperative was founded in 1961 under
the direction of Father Henri Tardy. While a little carving and
sealskin tapestry sewing had been done in Holman as early as
the 1950s (and sold on an individual basis to the HBC and to
the occasional tourist or government official who visited the
community), these handicrafts were not systematically mar-
keted in the South. Aware that the community desperately
needed additional sources of income, Father Tardy organized

the Holman Eskimo Cooperative to produce prints, carvings, and sealskin products. Tardy himself wrote (1979:69): "The villagers of Holman were in dire need of money. Tuberculosis was increasing, the igloo dwelling was inadequate. Trapping was poor, the white fox fur ridiculously low in price. There was no commercial value to seal pelts and fish nets were most expensive. To secure the necessities of life, I used to encourage our occasional visitor to buy a piece of local handicraft."

In 1961, Tardy was searching for a way to tan sealskins when he met Paul Godt, a co-op specialist working for the government. At Godt's suggestion, Tardy and five local people pooled ten dollars each to form the Holman Eskimo Cooperative on April 21, 1961. Once formed, the co-op was able to borrow money from the Eskimo Loan Fund in order to purchase and eventually to market carvings and sealskin rugs, tapestries, and purses made by Holman residents.

Soon after, while visiting a friend in Fort Smith, Tardy saw for the first time an Inuit print from Cape Dorset. Realizing that Holman artists were capable of producing similar works of art, Tardy started work on the Holman Eskimo Cooperative's first print collection. He was assisted by Helen Kalvak, Victor Ekootak, Harry Egotak, Alec Banksland (Peter Aliknak), Jimmy Memogana, and Wallace Goose, later joined by Patrick Akovak, Agnes Nanogak (Goose), Mona Ohoveluk, and Bill Goose. Their printmaking technique was primitive, utilizing a tanned sealskin stencil shaved with a razor. The image was then printed on a piece of paper by way of a fine grill and a toothbrush soaked in ink. In 1962, Holman's first small collection of prints was sent to Yellowknife and sold through the assistance of one of Tardy's friends. The initial, modest venture was successful. Tardy ordered more supplies to produce a second collection (Park 1990:17).

The Co-op

Elsie Nilgak. The co-op started off with prints, drawings, and by sewings—like small tapestries and purses with designs on them. But it was started mainly with drawings. The purses that we started with, we used to sew designs of our northern animals on them with a drawstring at the top. These purses were all made of sealskin. We also included designs of people with traditional clothing either hunting or dancing.

The craft shop was in one of those Quonset huts. One was

used for the co-op and the other was used for playing games in and dancing. They were built side by side right across from one another. They had one entrance by the center—like a porch connecting both buildings. You would enter by one door at the center, then turn either right or left to enter the co-op or the church-games building.

Then, after a couple of months, they ordered fabric materials such as burlap. That's when we started painting the drawings onto them with stone stencils. Then, we would sew the edges and fringe them. The materials came in throughout the summer. Although we weren't sewing all that much, that's how the co-op got started up. The co-op was mainly started up by Father Tardy and the artists who did the drawings.

Simon Kataoyak. The Holman Eskimo Co-op was started by Father Tardy back in 1961. The primary reason for starting it was to bring the two groups of people, Anglicans and Catholics, together. Since the community was divided, Father Tardy thought that a co-op would be the best way to get people to work together. The other reason the co-op was started was that there was nothing here in the way of jobs. People didn't have many ways to earn money. Father Tardy started the co-op with the help of a lay sister, Monique Piche. The co-op started mostly with the prints made by Jimmy Memo[gana], Alec Banksland, Harry Egotak, Kalvak, and Nanogak. Those five were the ones who really started the printmaking. Later, the co-op started making sewing like sealskin tapestries. The first board of directors was made up of Alec, Harry, Nanogak, Jimmy, Kalvak, and Taipana.

I started working for the co-op around 1963 as an assistant manager and bookkeeper. I had just come back from school in Yellowknife in 1961. In 1963, the work at the co-op was more than just Father Tardy and Monique Piche could handle, so I was hired for $5 a week. It wasn't much, but $5 could buy a lot of things in those days. Father Tardy worked as a manager of the co-op until about 1976 when Fred Van Duffelen was hired. Since Fred, we have had a lot of different co-op managers.

By March 1963, the printmakers of Holman had produced ten images for presentation to the Eskimo Arts Council in Ottawa—a body formed that year to approve and certify all Inuit artwork coming out of the North, to ensure that only high quality Inuit art reached the marketplace. To the dismay of Father Tardy and the Holman printmakers, the Holman collec-

Fig. 5.15. Jimmy Memogana working on stonecut print at co-op print shop, early 1960s.
The first Holman prints were produced using
either sealskin stencils or stonecuts. The stonecut technique involved carving the image on
a flat stone, usually a soft stone like soapstone.
This work required great skill and precision.
Once completed, the stone was inked and a
thin sheet of printing paper laid over it. The
printer then used a tool to press the paper
against the inked stone. This had to be done
carefully so that each of the fifty prints produced from one block would be identical.
Photo by Father Maurice Metayer. Courtesy of
the Holman Community Education Council.

tion was rejected in its entirety. The explanation was that too much "white influence" was evident in the prints. Members of the arts council mistakingly believed that Tardy had provided too much instruction to the printers as to what and how to draw. This white influence was also assumed from the perspective (or depth) that appeared in some of the drawings (Father Tardy, personal communication). Tardy was forced to return to Holman with the disheartening news that their work had been in vain. In a 1978 interview, Tardy said:

> This first [1963] collection was criticized because the south was a strong influence. We asked one man to do the collection. . . . Alex [Alec Banksland] worked night and day to do the collection. He did a few of the drawings and all of the printing himself. We played with the colour and the colour variations. . . . Alex is an Eskimo and has that [cultural] background. He is an Eskimo and an artist and he did them himself. I tried to explain to the Eskimo Arts Council that I had nothing to do with it; I'm not an artist (Tardy, in Sparling and Snowdon 1978).

Despite the arts council's rejection, Tardy and the Holman printers continued their efforts. In March 1964, the government sent an art advisor, Barry Coomber, to Holman in order to teach printmaking techniques. A recent graduate of the Ontario Arts College, Coomber introduced block printing, using local limestone, and initiated lithography and etching. The presence of an advisor provided the Holman Eskimo Cooperative with a degree of credibility with the government *and* the Eskimo Arts Council. In November 1965, the co-op presented a collection of thirty prints to the Eskimo Arts Council and it was enthusiastically received. Since 1965, the co-op's annual print collections have gained an international reputation and are a co-op staple.

In retrospect, it is ironic that the Eskimo Arts Council thought it acceptable for Holman artists to be exposed to "southern influence" through a formally trained art advisor but not through Father Tardy (who anyway denies having such an influence). Apparently, the notion of "southern influence" was selectively perceived by members of the council. The result, however, was that the 1965 print collection looked remarkably similar to prints produced at Cape Dorset (another successful printmaking community), which the arts council thought should be the model for all other northern communities. It would take years for the unique stenciling techniques used in Holman's 1963 collection to be resurrected at Holman. Today, however, Holman's printmakers are known for their superior stenciling abilities.[6]

In 1966, further experiments were done at the co-op to develop a technique for printing images on fabric. These experiments were initiated by Monique Piche, a Roman Catholic lay missionary who lived in Holman between 1963 and 1973. Piche helped to organize the co-op's craft shop production. The first technique involved a tile glued to a square wooden block. Drawings were carved into the tile, which was then inked with a roller and the image was printed on fabric using a rubber hammer (Monique Piche, personal communication, 1989). In the summer of 1966, Piche traveled to Ottawa to learn more about textile printing and silkscreening. The ultimate goal was to establish a small textile printing cottage industry that would provide employment to Holman residents. According to Piche: "It was evident that as the settlement grew, more and more people would leave their camp sites to move into the village, being attracted by the school, HBC store, and nursing station. It appeared necessary that if the children were kept busy going to school, the adults should also have something to do and have a way of earning their living" (Monique Piche, personal communication, 1989).

When Piche returned from Ottawa in the fall of 1966, further experimentation with designing and textile printing was done. A problem at the time was the marketing of finished products (wall hangings and placemats), since planes came into Holman only about once a month, but the following year the textile printing project got a big boost when the Hudson's Bay Company ordered large numbers of Holman placemats and wall-hangings. It was the year of the Montreal Exposition as well as the NWT's centenary celebration, and HBC expected Holman silkscreens to be excellent items to sell in its stores. To meet the Bay's order, the production of placemats and wallhangings began on a large scale, with five to ten women working full time at the craft shop. This order, in addition to the continued production of Holman prints, allowed the cooperative to establish itself and expand. As markets grew, the co-op added new

6. The 1963 print collection is stored in a fireproof vault at the print shop. During the summer of 1991, author Condon had an opportunity to view the collection with co-op manager Gordon Peters and Holman artists Mary Okheena and Elsie Klengenberg. We unanimously rated it as a superb collection, in both technique and design. It is hard to fathom why the Eskimo Arts Council rejected it.

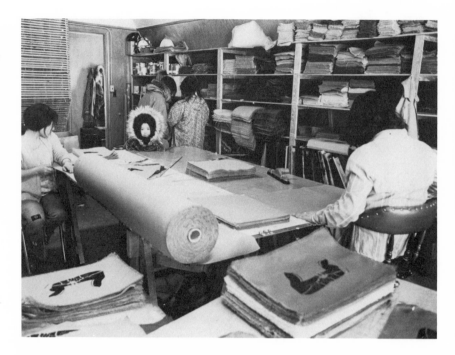

Fig. 5.16. Interior of Holman Eskimo Cooperative craft shop, mid-1970s. By the mid-1970s, the craft shop was producing a wide range of items for southern export, including Inuit parkas, boots, stone carvings, tablecloths, place mats, wall-hangings, book bags, and other items with Inuit designs. The women in this photograph are producing place mats by cutting pieces of fabric that will be silk-screened with an Inuit print. Photo by Tessa MacIntosh, © Native Communications Society of the NWT.

items to its production line. These items included new silk-screen products manufactured at the craft shop and sewn items that women produced at home. Marketing and shipping procedures eased in the early 1970s as scheduled air flights became more frequent (once a week in 1973).

In the late 1960s and early 1970s, the co-op diversified its activities. New projects included operating the Holman post office, providing oil delivery, and starting a small hotel and coffee shop. The latter was done by putting together three discarded matchbox houses. The hotel was created in order to meet the needs of a growing number of visitors, mostly government workers but also a few tourists. In 1972, Tardy decided that it was time for him to step down from the position of co-op manager and to allow Holman residents to assume total responsibility for the co-op. He wrote: "In 1972, time had come for the Eskimos to assume entirely the Co-op's responsibility. Simon Kataoyak, assistant manager, could take pride in saying that their co-op was the result of indomitable courage and lively Eskimo spirit. Their work was appreciated by the people of the South and remains a source of inspiration" (Henri Tardy 1979:75).

Since Tardy's departure as manager, the board of directors of the Holman cooperative has been completely responsible for setting policy and guiding the co-op's activities. Because the co-op had become such a large operation, it was necessary to hire, from the South, managers who were formally trained in business and management. With such help, the co-op has continued to expand. A new hotel was constructed in 1980 and expanded several years later. In 1985, fire completely destroyed the old craft shop, forcing the co-op to build a new and larger building. This new craft shop, named after Father Tardy, included space for the craft shop, a grocery/hardware store, co-op offices, and a post office.

The Move to Queen's Bay

In 1965, the federal government decided to relocate the growing Holman community to Queen's Bay. The original settlement site had an extremely rocky and rough terrain and government officials decided that this would seriously hamper expansion of the community. The gently sloping gravel surface of Queen's Bay, however, provided an ideal location.

In 1963 and 1964, the government shipped in seven more matchbox units (L-shaped units, slightly larger than the first Plan 370 units) and erected them on the shore of Queen's Bay. As a result, for several years the community of Holman was split between Queen's Bay and the old King's Bay site. In the spring of 1966, residents began the tedious process of jacking up all the remaining buildings at the King's Bay site, loading them onto large skids, and dragging them by bulldozer over the frozen ice of King's Bay. The process was especially difficult for the larger buildings, such as the Roman Catholic Mission Quonset huts and the Anglican Mission residence. Due to their size, these buildings had to be jacked up high enough that heavy-duty skids could be slipped underneath. They were then dragged, very slowly, by bulldozer (the first such piece of equip-

155

Fig. 5.17. Harry Egotak, Jimmy Memogana, and Alik Banksland preparing skid for Roman Catholic Mission Quonset hut. Photo by Father
Henri Tardy. Courtesy of the Holman Community Education Council.

ment to be shipped to Holman). According to Morris Nigiyok,
these larger buildings were dragged so slowly that he and other
workers passed the time by making and drinking tea inside
them as they were hauled over the ice. The move was not without its complications. The smaller of the two Roman Catholic
Quonset huts (which was being used at the time as a residence
by Father Tardy) was so heavy that the skids broke as it was
taken around the point separating Queen's Bay from King's
Bay. Tardy had to spend several nights sleeping in the Quonset
on the ice until repairs could be made to the skids. The Anglican
residence experienced similar problems. While being dragged
up on the beach of Queen's Bay, its skids stuck in the soft gravel
and the building was stranded for several days at an extreme
angle. The Anglican minister (probably Nigel Wilford) continued to use it.

Transport of the smaller buildings, such as the matchbox
residences and HBC warehouses, was quicker. While the larger
buildings had to be taken over the ice, around the point, the

Fig. 5.18. Roman Catholic Mission's Quonset hut Being moved on skids over King's Bay ice to new site on Queen's Bay. While the hut was being moved, the skids broke. Father Tardy, who lived in the hut, slept out of town in the stranded building for several nights until the skids were repaired. Photo by Father Tardy. Courtesy of the Holman Community Education Council.

Fig. 5.19. Pulling the HBC store building across King's Bay, 1966. The snowmobile on the left of the photo belonged to Father Tardy and was one of the first at Holman. Photo by Father Tardy. Courtesy of the Holman Community Education Council.

Fig. 5.20. Flossie Pappidluk and children (Margaret Kanayok, John Alikamek, and Effie Kataoyak) eating duck at Mashuyok, mid-1950s. Photo by Father Maurice Metayer. Courtesy of the Holman Community Education Council.

smaller ones were simply dragged up the steep hill on the west side of King's Bay.

Through today's eyes, the new settlement would have looked like nothing but a small cluster of residences dwarfed by the expansive gravel ridge upon which they were built. Nevertheless, by the end of 1966, the new settlement included, in addition to the buildings brought over from King's Bay, a federal day school, two teacher residences, a powerhouse, and a new Anglican church. The modernization and expansion of Holman had begun, and in a new location that could accommodate the needs of the growing population.

6. Modernization and Change in a Northern Community

The Queen's Bay Site, 1966 to the Present

ONCE RELOCATION of the community to the new site was complete, expansion of services and construction of newer and larger housing units occurred at a relatively rapid pace. Over the last 30 years, Holman has changed from an isolated trapping and trading outpost to a community articulated with the outside world through television, radio, fax machine, telephone, and almost daily air service. The pace of modernization since the founding of Holman in 1939 can be seen in the following table.

Social Change in Holman, 1939 to the Present:
A Chronology

1939	Founding of Holman on King's Bay site
1939 to 1967	Population gradually concentrates within the settlement
1941	Windcharger set up for Roman Catholic Mission
1943	Roman Catholic Mission purchases the *Mary*
1949	Father Tardy arrives in Holman to assist Father Buliard. Injured Buliard soon departs Holman
1961	Holman Eskimo Cooperative founded
1962	Small Anglican church constructed by local residents. Seven low-cost government houses

Fig. 6.1. *Juggling*, Holman Print Collection, 1984. Stonecut by Agnes Nanogak (artist) and Louie Nigiyok (printer). Edition: 50. Courtesy of the Holman Eskimo Cooperative.

	(matchboxes) constructed. Read Island HBC post closed. Bill Joss becomes new manager of Holman HBC post and some Read Island families move to Holman with Joss family
1963	First resident Anglican missionary, Rev. Bery Capron, arrives and is joined by fiancée Drina Staines, a registered nurse. The couple are married. Construction of Anglican residence. Roman Catholic Mission erects two large Quonset huts, starts kindergarten with two recently arrived lay sisters
1963 to 1964	Construction of low-cost, L-shape government houses on Queen's Bay site
1965	First snowmobile purchased by Father Tardy.
1966	Buildings moved from King's Bay to new site on Queen's Bay. Construction of federal day

	school and two teacher residences. Construction of new, larger Anglican church
1967	Construction of larger (3-bedroom) government housing units. Malgokak family moves to Holman from Berkeley Point—the last family to move in off the land
1970s	Electricity introduced to government housing. Polar bear sports hunting instituted.
1970 to 1972	Dog teams drop out of use, to be replaced by snowmobiles.
1972	Nursing station construction; first full-time nurse arrives. First Settlement Council established.
1977	Long-distance telephone service installed.
1978	Completion of airport runway and terminal. First privately owned car arrives—used by Pat Ekpakohak for a taxi service between town and airport. Ten new housing units, the first to have running water and flush toilets, completed.
1979	Co-op builds new hotel (Arctic Char Inn)
1980	New Hudson's Bay store constructed in center of town. Television and radio service installed
1982	Co-op celebrates twentieth anniversary and doubles hotel beds to eight. First Holman student graduates from high school in Yellowknife. Golf course constructed (three holes, later expanded to nine). A larger health center (named after Mark Emerak) constructed
1984	Holman given hamlet status; forms Hamlet Council.
1985	Helen Kalvak Ilihavik School constructed. Water pumphouse built at Air Force Lake
1988	New Hamlet offices built
1990	Construction of Ulukhaktok Recreation Centre, with indoor hockey rink and two curling rinks
1991	Hamlet records Holman population at 386
1993	New co-op arts and crafts shop opens

Examination of the table reveals the speed and extent of social change and the acceleration of change since the community moved to its present site. This chapter outlines the most significant developments since 1966 and provides a brief ethnographic sketch of contemporary settlement life. For a fuller account, readers are encouraged to consult *Inuit Behavior and Seasonal Change in the Canadian Arctic* (Condon 1983) and *Inuit Youth: Growth and Change in the Canadian Arctic* (Condon 1987).

Fig. 6.2. Old and new modes of transportation. Photo by Tessa Mac-
Intosh. © Native Communications Society of the NWT.

Both works provide technical details of settlement life from the
late 1970s to the mid-1980s.

The Snowmobile Revolution

Throughout most of the 1960s, dog-teams continued to be the
dominant mode of winter travel for hunting and trapping. The
first snowmobile in Holman was purchased by Father Tardy
around 1965 and soon afterward the HBC manager, Bill Joss,
purchased one, too. By 1970, the number of snowmobiles in
the community had increased to six, and hunters were using
them extensively for hunting and trapping. By 1972, dog-teams
had fallen into disuse as most hunters purchased Bombardiers,
Snow Cruisers, and Autoboggans.

Snowmobiles dramatically altered hunting practices. Because of the greater speed of snowmobiles, hunters could travel
much greater distances in search of game. Hunting and trapping trips that would have taken from several days up to a
week by dog-sled could now be accomplished in a fraction of
the time. Snowmobiles, combined with the use of high-powered

Fig. 6.3. ATVs driving down Ulukhaktok Bluff, 1987. Photo by John Paskievic. Courtesy of the Inuit Art Section, Indian and Northern Affairs Canada.

rifles, greatly increased efficiency. However, snowmobiles are expensive, both to purchase and to maintain, and the first such machines could be run only by individuals with access to substantial cash income or a good line of credit at the Bay. Moreover, snowmobiles were less reliable than dog teams, and frequent breakdowns were (and continue to be) a major problem. Lastly, while a hunter marooned in a blizzard could always eat his dogs if food supplies ran out, the snowmobile is universally regarded as unpalatable.

First Snowmobiles

Sam Oliktoak. The first snowmobiles were brought in by Bill Joss. Bill Joss, Allen Joss, and Jimmy Memogana were some of the first people to have snowmobiles [along with Father Tardy]. When Bill Joss brought them in, he was the manager of the store and the person who sold the first machines. The size of those first machines was fifteen horse. Those were the first machines used by people. Gradually, more machines came in over the years.

163

I got my first machine when my daughter, Lucy, was working at the nursing station and the school. She was the one who bought it. It was a four hundred. It had bogey wheels, track, but no sliders. So only the wheels kept it up from the ground. It was a lot better than dogs. When I went caribou hunting, it was so easy. You know a long time ago, dog-teams would scare away the caribou. When the dogs walked in the snow, that's when they scared the caribou. The caribou could hear the dog's qikaak [crunching sound in the snow] and the sound of the sleds. The caribou would run away so easily because of the sound. Back then, we always tried to hunt caribou only when it was windy and a little bit stormy. That's when we could get close to the caribou—when the caribou can't hear the dogs or sleds. We get close enough to see the caribou and they aren't running away. We leave the dogs behind and then walk up close enough to shoot. Sometimes the dogs would make other sounds that the caribou can hear. They can hear really well and would run away before we could get close. Even when it's windy and stormy, the caribou would run away sometimes. But the snowmobiles made hunting caribou a lot easier and faster.

Agnes Goose. The very first snowmobile here in Holman belonged to Father Tardy. When Father got that machine, it was real noisy. Boy, that Father! A short while after, other people started getting machines—like me and Wallace. We didn't know anything about Ski-Doos back then. Wallace and I got our first machine in the spring. We went out to Natkusiak's River when the rivers were starting to go. It was springtime, and we went over rocks, gravel, and even sunk into the mud. We tried so hard to pull the machine out, but it kept sinking back into the mud. We didn't know how to operate a machine then. Then we got it out of the mud and into the river. We let it spin and spin. We didn't know how to use it that's why. But that machine never broke down on us. People didn't know the difference whether it was broken or not, as long as it was still running. Those first Ski-Doos must have been pretty good. That's why people started using them.

Morris Nigiyok. Father Tardy got the first snowmobile. Seven horsepower. Boy, was it fast! Too fast. Then, Bill Joss came from Read Island with one. Then Tommy, then George. People started getting machines. My machine was a ten horse. My sister sent it. She gave it to me free. When I first started using that machine, I didn't take any supplies with me. I'd just get up and go. I didn't even take tools. Never thought about spare parts or anything like that. That's why I had to walk back from the other side of Minto once. The machine broke down. The points finished and no spare parts.

These factors notwithstanding, by the mid-1970s only a handful of dog-teams continued to be used in the Holman region, and this was mostly for recreational purposes. In the late 1970s, however, dog-teams made a significant comeback. Holman hunters and trappers started working as guides for polar bear sport-hunters and, since sports hunting of polar bears is not permitted from motorized vehicles, the hunters are taken out by dog-team.

The old Autoboggans and Snow Cruisers were scrapped long ago, to be replaced by high-speed and in some cases liquid-cooled Arctic Cats, Yamahas, and Ski-Doos. Most households now own at least one snowmobile, using it for hunting, running errands around town, and pleasure cruising. As the automobile is to southern society, so is the snowmobile in the North. In addition, since the mid-1980s all-terrain vehicles (ATVs) have increased in popularity among Holman residents. In the early 1980s, only one or two households owned such vehicles. Now, almost every household owns one. Before the days of the three- and four-wheeled ATVs, most summer travel on the tundra was done by walking, which greatly limited the distances people could travel for fishing or hunting. Now, a network of trails leads out from Holman to lakes in the surrounding area and any warm evening in June or July a stream of Holman residents heads out to fish with rod and reel.

Housing and Municipal Services

One of the most visible changes in the community has been in the type of housing and municipal services provided for Holman residents. As mentioned in chapter 5, immediately after the move to the Queen's Bay site, municipal services were not provided, but within several years basic amenities were arranged for under a contract system. Water was delivered to all housing units and garbage and sewage pick-up was organized.

In the late 1960s, the government changed its housing program: the small matchbox units had proved inadequate for the large Holman families. It was not uncommon for a family of

Fig. 6.4. Holman elder Albert Palvik sitting on ATV in front of his home, 1987. Photo by John Paskievic. Courtesy of the Inuit Art Section, Indian and Northern Affairs Canada.

nine or ten to be living in one of the small, early units. As a result, the government constructed a number of three-bedroom units for the larger families. Even in the early 1970s, these units must have seemed luxurious, both in terms of space and amenities, but by the standards of the 1990s they would be inconvenient, lacking running water, flush toilets, and adequate insulation.[1]

Housing in the 1970s

Joshua Oliktoak. It didn't seem like it was crowded. It was comfortable. But it was fun. There was always some family there.

1. The honey-bucket mode of waste disposal entails placing a thick plastic bag in a pail that is in turn placed inside a larger pail, which has a toilet seat on top. When full, the bag is sealed and placed outside to be hauled to the dump. Although the NWT Housing Corporation has been trying replace

Your parents would go out and there was always somebody there to take care of you. Sometimes you'd end up sleeping in a room with two or three people, but it was just a part of life. Today, when there are just even eight people in one house, it feels crowded. Not like long ago. It didn't feel crowded back then. There used to be eleven or twelve people in one house. I know my parents lived like that for a long time. There were lots of us that's why. It was good. Good life growing up like that. You'd learn from so many different people, different brothers and sisters. Not from just your parents. Maybe that has something to do with the way people are drifting apart today. The houses are twice as big as long ago and there's not even a quarter of the same amount of people in the same house. Long ago, even though it was crowded, it was just a part of life. It didn't seem crowded. It was fun.

In 1978 and 1979, however, the Housing Corporation of the NWT constructed thirteen houses (two, three, and four-bedroom units) with running water and flush toilets and since 1978 all units have been built with running water.

The advent of plumbing and internal septic and water tanks has placed a greater demand upon both maintenance requirements and municipal services. Since permafrost prevents the installation of water and sewage pipes underground, each house has been designed as a self-contained unit. Water trucks deliver water several times weekly, and a sewage truck pumps out the internal septic tanks on a similar schedule. As of 1994, with more than 120 housing units, the majority of which have running water, the water tankers must operate at an ever faster pace, although the construction of a pumphouse at Air Force Lake in 1985 has aided immensely in streamlining the process. Prior to 1985, water truck operators had to chisel holes in the lake ice before pumping water into the truck.

The housing situation in Holman has been improved through home-ownership programs begun in the mid-1980s. Under the first of these programs, Holman residents at a certain income level could qualify for HAP (Home Assistance Program) houses. The government supplied materials and a small amount of cash to assist in house construction. Ownership of the house transfered to the occupant after five years. This successful pro-

honey-buckets with flush toilets, a number of older housing still use the honey-bucket system.

Fig. 6.5. Shannon and Lillian Kanayok with their grandmother, Flossie Pappidluk, 1987. In the mid-1980s, the Housing Corporation of the NWT built a number of apartment units (four-plexes) to provide for the housing needs of single elders and young unmarried men and women. Photo by John Paskievic. Courtesy of the Inuit Art Section, Indian and Northern Affairs Canada.

gram encouraged numerous people to build and maintain homes and in the summer of 1993 Holman had nineteen HAP houses. That program had since been replaced by the ACCESS program, which is operated by the Housing Corporation of the NWT. Families that qualify purchase houses on a fifteen-year mortgage, adjusted to income. As of the summer of 1994, one ACCESS house was under construction and five more were scheduled.

Political Development

As Holman has grown and become inextricably articulated with the outside world, so has grown the need for a more developed

Fig. 6.6. David Kanayok filling water truck at Air Force Lake, using new pump station, summer 1991. Photo by Richard G. Condon.

local self-government. Until the early 1970s, there was no self-government in the community. All government administration was handled by non-Inuit—first the Coppermine RCMP, then the Holman school principal (from circa 1966 to 1969), and then a resident government administrator (approximately 1969 to 1972). In 1972, the NWT Department of Local Government sent Kane Tologanak to help organize Holman's first settlement council—a body viewed by NWT officials as a necessary first step in encouraging community responsibility for local government. In the first election, which generated a great deal of interest on the part of local residents, twelve people ran for seven seats (Kane Tologanak, personal communication). The first chairman of the council was Simon Kataoyak, and Bill Goose was the first settlement secretary. In the early days of the council, funding was quite limited. The maximum a settlement council could receive and spend was $12,000, which had to cover all expenses. The council also qualified for recreation grants of $5 per person. Although the settlement council was a significant initial step to the development of local government, the council was extremely limited in what it could accomplish. It could not pass by-laws, could not generate revenue, could not administer grants, and could not set its own budget.

Local Government

Kane Tologonak. I was working for the Department of Local Government in the early 1970s, and one of our primary goals was organizing settlement councils. We organized the first settlement council here in 1972. We organized it and quite a few people ran for the seven seats. We had about twelve people running for those seven seats. All of them were notable people in the community. People were really interested in it. The first chairman was Simon Kataoyak, and Bill Goose was the first settlement secretary. That's when the co-op was running the little coffee shop and transient center that's being used as a warehouse now. That was the hangout. That's where I took most of the people's pictures. They'd come over and I'd take their picture and we set up the ballots with pictures on it so people who couldn't read could put their *X* beside the person they wanted to vote for.

In those days, funding was limited. The maximum that a settlement could get was twelve thousand dollars to run a community. That was to cover everything. Also they got a per capita recreation grant which was five dollars per person. In those days, it didn't cost that much to put things on. Now they have developed to the point that they are a Hamlet Council. In twelve years, they've gone quite a ways.

The hamlet council has a lot more money, but has more expenses as well. They have to be more careful, responsible, and accountable for their spending. But they decide how to spend it. As a hamlet, they set up their own budget which they couldn't do before. They get a hamlet contribution of over four hundred thousand dollars from the government. Then there are other program like recreation grants and water-sewage programs where they can get more money.

In April 1984, Holman was incorporated as a hamlet. Under this form of government, Holman residents are able to elect a mayor and councilors who have much more control over financial matters. The Holman Hamlet Council can pass bylaws, apply for and administer municipal grants, and perform many functions not previously possible. For its new responsibilities (municipal services, road construction and improvement, heavy-duty equipment maintenance, airport maintenance, sports and recreation, alcohol and drug education, community planning, and more), Holman has a significantly larger budget. In 1994, total operating expenditures exceeded $2.2 million, a far cry from that first council's minuscule operating budget of $12,000. The municipality is the single largest employer in the community (twenty-five to thirty people in summer 1994) and boasts a new office building (built in 1988) and located in the center of town.

Another significant political development in the Holman region has been the settlement of land claims with the federal government of Canada. As in many areas of the North American Arctic, land claims negotiations have been a long, tedious process. A number of developments in the early 1970s led to the initiation of the land claims process in northern Canada. The first and most obvious of these was the signing of the Alaska Native Claims Settlement Act (1971) which called attention to the noticeable lack of such negotiations in Canada. This was followed by the signing of the James Bay and Northern Quebec Agreement, paving the way to Phase I of the large James Bay hydroelectric project.

In May 1977, the Committee for Original People's Entitlement, representing the Inuit (Inuvialuit) communities of the western Canadian Arctic (including Holman), submitted a formal land claim to the federal government entitled Inuvialuit Nunangat. Negotiations continued into the first part of 1978, culminating in the signing of an Agreement in Principle that October. Both parties agreed that a final agreement would be signed within a year, but government intransigence and a high turnover in personnel resulted in significant delays. In 1984 the process was completed and Holman residents became beneficiaries of the Western Arctic Land Claim agreement (also known as the Inuvialuit Final Agreement).

Under the agreement, residents of Holman and the five other Inuvialuit communities (Paulatuk, Sachs Harbour, Tuktoyaktuk, Inuvik, and Aklavik) have relinquished aboriginal claims to traditional territories in exchange for a cash settlement and exclusive proprietary rights to 35,000 square miles of land close to the six communities participating in the claim. In each of the communities, a distinction is made between 7(1)(a) lands and 7(1)(b) lands. In 7(1)(a) lands, the beneficiaries hold both surface and subsurface rights, while in 7(1)(b) lands, only surface rights are held. The land claim also allowed for the creation

VICTORIA

ISLAND

7(1)(a)

HOLMAN

0   32mi.
Scale

Map 11. Inuvialuit land claims. Holman land
selection for Unuvialuit Final Agreement showing 7(1)(a) (the area shaded with dots) and
7(1)(b) (diagonal shading) lands (source: page
96 of *The Western Arctic Claim: The Inuvialuit
Final Agreement.* Indian and Northern Affairs
Canada, Government of Canada, Ottawa, 1984).

of a regional development corporation (Inuvialuit Development
Corporation) as well as individual community corporations
(such as the Holman Community Corporation). All of these corporations are involved in economic development projects (at
either the regional or local level) and social service and cultural
programs.

Contemporary Economic Adaptation

As Holman has increased in size and complexity, the economic
base of the community has become much more varied. As described earlier, until the 1970s most Holman residents supported themselves by subsistence hunting, trapping, limited

arts and crafts production, and modest amounts of social assistance. Over the last two decades, more opportunities have become available. As the reputation of the Holman Eskimo Cooperative has grown, so have the opportunities for employment in arts and crafts production. In addition, as the community has grown, so has the number of service and administrative positions in housing, health care, local government, municipal services, retail sales, and education. The Holman economy now has overlapping and constantly evolving sectors: 1. subsistence hunting; 2. trading in renewable resources (the products of trapping, commercial fishing, and hunting); 3. wage employment; 4. sports guiding; 5. arts and crafts production; 6. private enterprise; 7. social assistance.

Economic Change

Gary Bristow. When I first came to Holman, this was a much more traditional community. Most of the money in the community came from hunting and trapping. You could go out and trap and do fairly well twenty years ago. And it had been that way for years. It all started to fall apart with the banning of seals and other things. It killed the market. When I was working for the Hudson's Bay Company in 1979, I was paying twenty dollars per sealskin, any kind of sealskin. I would buy as many as I could. I bought seventeen hundred in one month. I spent in excess of thirty thousand dollars just buying sealskins. In 1991 and 1992, the Bay actually quit buying seals. They don't buy sealskins anymore. The co-op buys selectively, in the order of one hundred to two hundred a year. Fox prices in 1991 and 1992 were down to five dollars each. Last year, they were up a little bit, up to twenty-five dollars, which is reasonable. But I think there was a loss with some of the younger generation who are now around twenty-five years old. The traditional way of life was still good while most of them were growing up. There was no real push for them to get an education or anything else. Now that the traditional way of life is gone and they have no education, they're kind of stuck. I think one of the problems in this community and other communities throughout the NWT is that the younger generation is stuck. I'd like to do something. Being realistic, I think if I can [as mayor] create one or maybe two new hamlet jobs a year, I'm doing well. Nowadays, the money just isn't there either.

Subsistence Hunting

Despite the increasing reliance on imported foodstuffs, subsistence hunting and fishing continue to play an important role in the local economy. Residents of Holman are fortunate to live in a region of the Arctic which is generally acknowledged to be relatively abundant in fish, caribou, musk ox, polar bear, seals, and waterfowl. For many households, subsistence hunting and fishing remain the primary sources of food and some clothing. Although wage-earning households generate income which can be used to purchase southern foods at the store, there is nevertheless a preference for fresh "land" foods over expensive canned goods, frozen meats, and microwave dinners. In fact, many of the active hunters are wage earners who must limit their hunting trips to weekends and on holidays.

The sharing of "land" foods continues to be important in Inuit social relations. Foods obtained from subsistence hunting are usually shared. An active hunter will not only provide for his or her own family, but will provide food to related households. This reflects the Inuit recognition of social interdependence between families and households, as well as the fact that the

Fig. 6.7. Simon Kataoyak hunting seal at the ice edge, November 1979. Photo by Richard G. Condon.

eating and sharing of land foods (or real food, as Inuit are likely to describe it) is an essential ingredient in the definition of Inuit identity.

Despite this preference, there is an overall trend away from subsistence hunting/fishing as the dominant economic activity. In increasing numbers of young households, hunting and fishing are done only sporadically. The availability of other forms of employment combined with the very high cost of purchasing equipment for subsistence hunting (snowmobiles, rifles, sleds, camping gear, gasoline, oil, and so forth) stops many young people from embarking on hunting or fishing with any substantial commitment. Moreover, many young people do not have the skills required for survival on the land. This has been a cause for concern among many elder hunters, who fear the loss of traditional knowledge among the younger generation.

Fig. 6.8. Richard and David Notaina unloading insulation for outpost camp at Omingmagiuk, north shore of Minto Inlet, 1979. In the mid- to late 1970s, a number of Holman hunters and trappers, funded by NWT grants, established outpost camps—one at Halahiqvik on the north shore of the sound (one hundred miles to the east of Holman), the other at Omingmagiuk. Both were abandoned in the late 1980s due to falling prices for furs. Photo by Richard Condon.

Since the 1930s and 1940s, trapping of white fox has been an essential part of the Holman economy and has provided a significant portion of income for many families. In the 1960s, the trading of sealskins added another income source to the economy. Before the 1960s and 1970s, most able-bodied men in the community engaged in fox trapping and seal hunting, at least to some degree, largely because access to other sources of income was extremely limited. In the 1980s, increasing pressure from animal rights groups and antitrapping organizations undermined the international market for furs and skins and today the amount of trapping and seal hunting in the Holman region is relatively negligible. Few young people in the community express any desire to become involved in such demanding work.

Despite the decline of trapping and seal hunting, a number of other activities that exploit the renewable resources of the area have been developed. For example, these include the netting of arctic char and the harvesting of musk ox, both of which may be sold locally (usually to the Arctic Char Inn) or exported to restaurants in Yellowknife and elsewhere. Both the fishing and musk ox harvesting are done within limits to prevent overexploitation of the resource, but they provide some income to local hunters and fishermen. Recently, the co-op started buying musk ox qiviut (wool) from Holman hunters for sale to weavers outside the community for the hand-weaving of sweaters and scarves.

Wage Employment

Since the early 1960s, there has been a gradual expansion of employment opportunities and today wage employment ranges from high-paying salaried jobs in the government sector (which usually require advanced education and training) to relatively low-paying part-time and casual jobs. Summer sees a significant increase in casual employment as construction and maintenance projects are initiated. Such projects may include community clean-up, road construction, house building or renovation, painting, and other general maintenance chores.

Although the past ten years have seen an increase in the number of high-paying salaried positions, the rate of population growth has meant that not every qualified individual will obtain one of these highly desirable positions. Competition for

salaried jobs has become more intense and many trained individuals have had to settle for jobs far below their level or move
to other communities. Many in the younger generation prefer
to tolerate unemployment or underemployment in order to remain in Holman, which is regarded as one of the more livable
communities in the NWT.

Sports Guiding

Since the mid-1970s, the guiding of sport hunters has become
an important source of income, most notably for older Inuit
whose traditional hunting and trapping livelihoods have been
undermined by the anti-fur movement (see Wenzel 1991 for a
recent discussion of the animals rights movement and its impact upon Canadian Inuit). In the spring and fall, sport hunters
from all over the world visit Holman to hunt caribou, musk
ox, and polar bear. These hunts are coordinated by the Holman
Hunters and Trappers Association, usually in conjunction with
outfitters in southern Canada.

The sport hunters pay large sums of money to obtain their

Fig. 6.9. Holman guides preparing to Take a sportsman out to hunt
polar bear, 1980. Photo by Richard G. Condon.

177

trophy animals. The most highly prized and expensive trophy animal is, of course, the polar bear. The hunting of polar bears is heavily regulated by the federal government and there are strict limits on the number of polar bears that can be harvested in each community. Holman hunters usually receive approximately twenty to twenty-four polar bear tags per year. Some of these tags (the number varies from year to year) are reserved by the local hunter and trapper association for sports hunters. Federal hunting regulations also specify that all polar bear sport hunters must be taken out by dog-team. Usually two teams and two guides accompany each hunter. In addition to providing income, the sport hunts have revived the use of dog-teams.

Arts and Crafts

Since the incorporation of the Holman Eskimo Cooperative in the early 1960s, arts and crafts production has been a vital

Fig. 6.10. Mabel Nigiyok displays a print at Holman print shop, 1987. Photo by John Paskievic. Courtesy of the Inuit Art Section, Indian and Northern Affairs Canada.

178

Fig. 6.11. Louie Nigiyok and Peter Palvik working at print shop, 1987. Photo by John Paskievic. Courtesy of the Inuit Art Section, Indian and Northern Affairs Canada.

source of income to Holman as well as an important outlet for creative expression. Holman carvings and prints are on display at some of Canada's finest museums. The co-op still organizes most of the community's printing, carving, and crafts production, but an increasing number of artists and craftsmen are producing and marketing their works independently.

Working at the Print Shop

Mabel Nigiyok. Long ago, when the co-op was built in Holman, I did not know what it was. When I was asked to sew for the craft shop, I did not know what I was supposed to do. Later, when I learned what the co-op was for, I began sewing sealskin articles. That's when the craft shop used to be situated across King's Bay.

179

It was there I heard about people making carvings and prints, but I did not take notice of them. In my mind they did not seem important. When I was asked to make a drawing, I tried, although my drawing did not resemble anything. They looked very funny. I thought very hard as to what I would draw about. I brought the drawing to the co-op. When I showed the drawing, I was very shy and nervous, so they told me to keep trying. After that I didn't draw for a number of years. I was looking after my children. I also had an adopted daughter at that time.

In 1981 I started working at the print shop. When I first walked in there I didn't know what to do. At that time, Elsie Klengenberg and I were working together. We didn't have any training. We learned by watching other people working and finishing up their work which was supposed to be done. At that time, there were no shadings on the prints. Elsie and I would discuss how to put shadings on them, and it was the first time there was a change on the prints. When I first started working, I used to do other people's drawings. I started drawing on my own. I'd draw what my parents went through long ago.

When I was a child, my parents lived in igloos. My parents did a lot of hunting and living off the land. That is how I was brought up. I draw what the elders told me about in those days. When I draw, I have to think hard in order to make a nice print. I am the eldest from my co-workers. I am fifty-six years old now. I like my work; it really helps me and my family a lot. In spring and summer I go out on the land for three months. [From the introduction to the 1994 Holman print catalogue, Holman, NWT].

Mary Okheena. I first started working at the print shop in 1977. I started with stencil printing. I was the only person in the art shop stencil printing at that time. My first stencils were out of paper. It's almost like tracing paper. We don't have them any more. You'd put a copper plate in the oven at four hundred degrees for about half an hour. You'd take it out and then get a candle and melt the wax on top of the copper and put the paper on top. Then take the paper off and cool it until it gets stiff. We would use those for stencils. It was lots of work. I had to make lots of those because they're not like these new ones. They would wear out. Sometimes, I would make three new stencils for just one print. Like here you don't have to make another one. Now, everything seems to go a little faster. The mylar, papers, and brushes have all changed.

We do a lot of different shadings now that we didn't do before. Now we do almost an airbrush stroke. When we started, we just did tapping. Now, we go back and forth. We've learned a lot more about where shadings should go in the art work.

When I'm traveling around to do my printwork and that, people always ask me when our printmaking techniques changed. They say that the old catalogues just show stonecuts, and there's no more stonecuts, only woodcuts. The woodcuts started around the middle of the 1980s. That's when they quit using stone and started using wood. I think it had something to do with health— you know, because the dust of the stone.

To me the printing industry is really important. The co-op is doing a lot of things now to make money. I don't think they'll quit doing the art work. They almost stopped one year. That was around 1985, 1986, 1987, around there. That's when the co-op was losing money. For some reason, they decided to keep doing the art work.

In the early eighties, we stopped going through the Eskimo Arts Council. I didn't like it when I used to go down for their meetings, when they would pick out the prints to be printed for the year. A lot of prints that they rejected were the prints that some tourists and visitors would really like. Those people would come around and see the proofs and say "Wow! What time is this print going to come out and how much is it going to cost?" We'd tell them we have no idea. Then the Arts Council would reject all these prints that some people really liked. It made me feel real mad and I want to tell them this and that, but I couldn't say anything.

What we usually do now after quitting the Arts Council is make all these proofs and get the titles and stories and hang them up in one room. We get all the stories and titles for the prints and then decide that this one has to change a little. Then we pick out the prints we want. It's a lot better than having an Arts Council since we use the prints we really like.

I like attending the openings in the South because you learn a lot of new things from people, like what they think of Holman art work and what they don't like. And these art critics tell you all these different things about what they think of the prints. It's really interesting. They give you a lot of things to think about.

Private Enterprise

The size and relative isolation of the community has severely limited opportunities for Holman residents to start and run their own businesses. Nevertheless, since the late 1970s, entrepreneurs have started a variety of enterprises, among them a taxi service, a shipping company (to and from the airport), a construction firm, a games arcade, an engine repair shop, and a snack bar. While the amount of income generated from private enterprise is negligible compared with that from other activity, these businesses will undoubtedly grow and earn more as the community expands.

Social Assistance

In spite of greatly expanded employment opportunities, the growing Holman population continues to outstrip manpower needs. This demographic dilemma plagues other northern communities, too. Fewer and fewer people are able to find suitable employment, forcing them to move elsewhere or rely on social assistance. In addition, many Holman hunters and trappers have become increasingly dependent on government transfer payments to make up for income lost as a result of the collapse of the fur market. Among all age categories, there has been a significant increase in all forms of social assistance in the last decade. This becomes even more apparent as the younger generation of Inuit comes of age with few employment opportunities available.

In sum, the Holman economy, like that of other northern communities, is both fragile and complex. Few families support themselves solely by one activity, but engage in a range of economic pursuits. In many respects, contemporary economic strategies retain the high degree of flexibility and opportunism that characterized traditional Copper Inuit society.

Transportation and Communication

During the 1950s and 1960s, flying in and out of the community was possible only on a sporadic basis, on the occasional Hudson's Bay Company, Roman Catholic, or government charters. In the early 1970s, weekly air service was initiated and this gradually expanded to twice-weekly service in the late 1970s. Today, Holman, with a modern transportation and communication system, is well connected with the world outside and travel to and from the community is relatively simple, albeit somewhat expensive.

Until 1978, planes continued to land on the Queen's Bay airstrip, which ran right down the center of town. For twelve

Fig. 6.12. Wardair plane on old airstrip, August 1978. Until the completion of the new airstrip in September of 1978, planes landed on a gravel airstrip that ran through the center of town. Photo by John Rose.

years, Holman residents were able to meet the airplane quite literally at their doorsteps. Recognizing the hazards of such a situation, (among them the fact that numbers of children were wandering onto the airstrip), the Canadian Department of Transportation built a new runway three miles to the west of town. Construction of the airport provided employment for a large number of Holman residents during 1977 and 1978, and the airport officially opened in the late summer of 1978. With the longer runway, larger aircraft were able to fly into the community with both passengers and supplies. By the summer of 1991, two airlines were flying scheduled air service, providing a total of five flights per week, not including charters for events such as the Kingalik Jamboree or the Billy Joss Invitational Golf Tournament.

The only other means of transportation into the community is via the annual barge, which arrives in late summer bearing heating oil, gasoline, building materials, and nonperishable foodstuffs. Frequently, snowmobiles and trucks are unloaded from the barge destined for government garages, the Bay, the co-op, or the hands of private individuals. The barge originates in Hay River, close to transportation networks linked to Edmonton, and travels down the Mackenzie River to Tuktoyaktuk, whence it sails eastward to Holman. Barge-time is one of the more exciting and hectic events of the year. Tons of equipment

Fig. 6.13. The barge preparing for unloading at King's Bay, September 1979. The barge calls at Holman only once a year. Photo by Richard G. Condon.

and supplies must be offloaded quickly so the barge can make other stops during the brief period in which waters are navigable.

Articulation with the outside world is also accomplished via two satellite dishes: one for television reception and the other for telephone service. Before Northwest Telephone installed a satellite dish in Holman, voice communication with the outside was limited to notoriously unreliable radio phones. In 1977, long-distance telephone service was installed, allowing Holman residents to call just about anywhere in the world. Today, direct-dialing is available to neighboring communities and all exchanges in the United States and Canada.

The satellite television receiver, installed in the fall of 1980, provided Holman residents with a single television station. Within a few years, however, the number of television channels was expanded from one to five. This was a significant step in breaking the barriers of isolation which shielded the community from developments in the outside world. With television, Holman residents can now get territorial, national, and international news as it occurs, rather than having to wait days or even weeks for newspapers and magazines to arrive by plane.

Most of the programs beamed into the community are from southern Canada and the United States; hence the dominant language is English. A limited number of news, information, and cultural programs are offered in Inuktituk, mostly emanating from the eastern Arctic (CBC North studios in Iqaluit).

The introduction of television has had a profound influence on community life. Although television has increased the level of awareness concerning the outside world, making people much more cosmopolitan in their outlook, it has also undermined traditional patterns of social visiting between households. Prior to 1980, visiting was the primary social/recreational activity, especially during the midwinter months of darkness and confinement. In the course of an evening, it would not be unusual for an individual or a couple to visit four or five households. Visiting provided opportunities for exchanging information and cementing social bonds within the village. In fact, prior to 1980, southern visitors to the community were most impressed by the relaxed and highly informal nature of social visiting, which was almost always accomplished without invitation or even a knock at the door. Television has especially increased social isolation between unrelated or distantly related households and visiting is no longer the dominant social activity. People now tend to watch television in the comfort of their own homes or participate in sports and other recreational activities at the school gym or the hockey arena.

As in any rapidly modernizing community, young people appear to have been the most dramatically impacted by television programming. Along with southern-style schooling, television has helped to alter their behavior, aspirations, outlook on life, and speech. English language dominates, and since many television programs are either about or oriented toward southern teenagers, Holman youths have gradually acquired the norms of southern youth culture.[2]

Community Health

In the 1950s and 1960s, the Inuit of Holman and other northern communities were ravaged by high infant-mortality rates and infectious diseases such as influenza and tuberculosis. In 1956, for example, 1,578 Inuit from the Canadian North lived in southern sanatoria, undergoing TB treatment (Condon 1983:99).

2. For more information on contemporary Inuit youth, see Condon 1987.

These patients constituted approximately 14 percent of the Inuit population in Canada. As the federal government stepped up vaccination of infants and children, in addition to isolating and treating infected individuals in southern hospitals, the number of active TB cases dropped dramatically. Similarly, the prenatal and postnatal health care has significantly reduced the Inuit infant-mortality rate, once the highest of any group in Canada.

These advances in Inuit health have been made possible by a variety of government health programs, including the opening of health clinics and nursing stations in northern communities in the 1960s and early 1970s. Prior to the construction of the Holman Nursing Station in 1972, all medical care at Holman was provided by either missionaries, a lay dispenser, or nurses from Coppermine, who periodically visited the community. Once the nursing station was completed, a full-time nurse was posted at Holman. In addition to responsibility for general community health, the nursing station also coordinated special programs, including a maternal health program, a preschool program, a tuberculosis program, a school health program, a chronic disease program, and an environmental sanitation program.

By the early 1980s, with the nursing station no longer adequate to meet the needs of the expanding population, Health and Welfare Canada built a larger nursing station (named in honor of Mark Emerak, the respected Holman elder and artist who died in 1983). The new Emerak Health Center has larger and better equipped facilities, two resident nurses, a housekeeper, a medical interpreter, a maintenance man, and a community health representative. The nurses are able to treat most ailments, but severe cases continue to be evacuated to Edmonton or Yellowknife, the territorial capital. Expectant mothers are sent out several weeks before their due dates. Although the health facility is equipped to manage births, Northern Medical Services prefers that, in the event of unforeseen complications, mothers give birth in hospital.

Education

With the construction of the federal day school on the new settlement site in 1966, young people were no longer required to leave Holman for their formal education from kindergarten through grade nine. This first school was a double-wide trailer

186

that could be divided into two classroom spaces. In addition, two housing units were built close to the school for occupation by teachers recruited from southern Canada. All schooling was in English, utilizing a curriculum based on that of the province of Alberta. Throughout the 1960s and 1970s, as the school-age population expanded, more trailer units were added and by 1978 the school complex consisted of four separate buildings: three classroom buildings and a combination workshop/kitchen. The school staff consisted of four white teachers, two Inuit classroom assistants, and a maintenance man.

Modern Education

Joshua Oliktoak. Schooling has really changed from when I was going to school. There's a lot better education. Teachers are more dependable. Maybe because they're paid better than long ago for coming all the way up here from all the way down south. They're staying longer too. Long ago teachers used to come for a year or two. They might not like it, but they'd stay until the end of the school year and then leave. Now they stay longer and get to know the students and their families. They end up getting close to the students and teaching them better. Attendance is better too. Over the past few years, there have been a lot more kids graduating high school, but they don't seem to be doing anything. They come back to town and end up getting low-paying jobs—what they'd end up doing anyway. If some of them went to university or college, maybe some of them would get a good job but that's a long time for them to go to school.

Two major problems that plagued the early years of the Holman school were poor attendance and academic underachievement. Attendance was relatively good in the younger grades, but dropped off dramatically in the upper grades. Averaged across all grade levels, attendance typically did not exceed 50 to 60 percent. Due to the cultural gap between school and home, many children were ill-prepared for the kinds of demands made upon them, and the school, with its southern-based curriculum, was viewed as a foreign entity.

One consequence of stresses experienced by teachers in their attempts to deal with low attendance, poor academic preparation, and greatly varied academic levels in one classroom was high teacher turnover. Often, before a teacher fully adjusted to

187

northern life and made accommodations to the learning needs of Inuit children, he or she would leave.

Schooling was provided up to grade nine. Thereafter, students wishing to complete high school had to spend three years at Sir John Franklin High School in Yellowknife. During the 1970s, no student successfully completed the three-year course of study at Yellowknife, which was perceived to be a strange, impersonal environment. Often, Holman students would quit within a few weeks or months because of homesickness and inadequate academic preparation. By winter 1982, only one student from Holman had completed the three-year course and received a high-school certificate. However, as Holman students became increasingly motivated and better prepared, the number of graduates increased. By 1988, seven students had graduated and the number has since slowly increased.

The school's four buildings were inadequate and in 1985 they were replaced by a large, imposing complex named for Helen Kalvak, the Holman artist. The Helen Kalvak School, the largest structure in the community, offers a comfortable and stimulating environment for learning. In addition to having modern classrooms, it contains a library, workshop, adult-education room, home economics room, spacious offices, and a gymnasium. School attendance has improved markedly since

Fig. 6.14. Baseball game in Holman, 1987. Photo by John Paskievic. Courtesy of the Inuit Art Section, Indian and Northern Affairs Canada.

the opening in the fall of 1985, as has the academic performance of students.

There are no formal grades beyond grade nine, but an adult-education program has been run since the 1986/1987 school year. Many students continue their educations at high schools in either Cambridge Bay or Coppermine (Sir John Franklin in Yellowknife no longer being an option), but a number decide to remain in the community and take adult education. The program was established to provide upgrading for adults (many of them seeking job advancement) but young people also attend, after waiting the required year to qualify.

The school curriculum continues to be based primarily on a southern model, but attempts are being made to introduce culturally relevant instructional materials, including Inuinnaqtun language instruction. Equally important is the fact that the Community Education Council (the CEC—formerly the Local Education Authority) has evolved to the point where it has more control over local education. The elected members of the CEC have significant input in the hiring of teachers, expenditure of funds, and selection of instructional materials. Local control of education also extends to regional level through the Kitikmeot Board of Education, which is made up of representatives from member CECs.

In 1994, there were nine full-time school employees and one

Fig. 6.15. Louisa Nigiyok, Kimberly "Uqalitana" Condon (author's daughter), and Louie Nigiyok at Holman golf course, the world's northernmost permanent nine-hole golf course, summer 1991. Photo by Richard G. Condon.

Fig. 6.16. White fox skins drying on a line, 1981. Photo by John Rose.

Fig. 6.17. Young Holman residents playing hockey at the outdoor hockey arena, 1988. Photo by Richard G. Condon.

Fig. 6.18. Agnes Nereyok making smoked tea, 1987. Photo by John Paskievic. Courtesy of the Inuit Art Section, Indian and Northern Affairs Canada.

part-time. Most of the certified teachers at Holman continue to be whites from southern Canada, but as of 1994 one Holman resident has completed teacher training and is now fully certified. Other Inuit teachers and counselors have undergone training to improve their skills.

Recreation

A few years after the move from King's Bay to Queen's Bay, a community hall was erected at the north end of the village. This multipurpose hall was used throughout the 1970s and 1980s for dances, meetings, games, movies, sporting events, and other community events. Due to the large size of the structure and a lack of adequate funding to pay for heating oil, the hall was often closed during much of the winter and recreational activity was largely limited to social visiting and the playing of card and board games. Teenagers frequently com-

Fig. 6.19. Harry Egotak, Sam Oliktoak, William Kagyut, and Jimmy Kudlak at Anglican service, 1987. Photo by John Paskievic. Courtesy of the Inuit Art Section, Indian and Northern Affairs Canada.

plained during the late 1970s that Holman was a boring place. Today, such complaints are rarely voiced. Holman excels in the organization of recreational and sporting activities. The Sports and Recreation Office of the Holman Hamlet Council, created in 1984, operates an extensive program of sports, games, athletic workshops, and tournaments. There is a substantial budget ($284,000 in 1994) and a full-time staff of four with two seasonal aides. Current recreational facilities in Holman include an indoor gymnasium attached to the school, two well-manicured baseball diamonds, the nine-hole golf course (the world's most northern), an outdoor hockey arena, an indoor hockey arena with locker rooms and a snack bar, and two indoor curling rinks.[3] Funding for sporting and recreational activities is received from the Holman Hamlet Council and through

3. The gymnasium is used for physical education classes during school hours. In the evenings it is operated by the Office of Sports and Recreation as venue for basketball, volleyball, dodge-ball, floor-hockey, and so forth.

192

Fig. 6.20. Esau Elgayak repairing komatik (sled) outside his home, 1987. Photo by John Paskievic. Courtesy of the Inuit Art Section, Indian and Northern Affairs Canada.

grants from the NWT government. Throughout the year, activities are organized for all age groups by Sports and Recreation. These include hockey, curling, baseball, golf, basketball, floor-hockey, and volleyball. The Office of Sports and Recreation also organizes competitions with neighboring communities. The Billy Joss Invitational Golf Tournament has attracted Edmonton Oilers hockey players as well as professional golfers from southern Canada.

Recreation

Joshua Oliktoak. Recreation has changed lots. There used to be no facilities when I was growing up. Just a community hall which was pretty small compared to gyms today. There was just a plywood floor. Now there's a real wood gym floor. Now there's an arena, curling rink, golf course, and ball diamonds. All those

Fig. 6.21. Jimmy Kudlak and granddaughter Trishia Ogina in front of their home, 1987. Photo by John Paskievic. Courtesy of the Inuit Art Section, Indian and Northern Affairs Canada.

things we didn't have when we were growing up. Lots of things. The arena is popular when it's open. It seems that's where most people go during the cold months of the year. Just about every other night, there's a hockey game going on. And there's lots of people up there. It's good for the people alright. All sorts of people. Recreation has been mostly good for the community. The only bad thing is that it makes people forget about what they used to do before they had all these facilities. Now, they're not doing all the things they used to do, and it takes away the closeness. It's too competitive now. It's not as much fun as it used to be. I think it's partly to do with all the facilities and programs that have come up here. That's why I was saying that a lot of good comes in but some good things go out too.

Gary Bristow. When I first came to Holman, we had no phones and no televisions. Back then, the big entertainment was playing cards and stuff like that. Now, when you go to visit, the TV is on all the time. It's the same all over, but it just took longer to get here. We've caught up a lot in that time. The quality of housing, for example, has really improved. When I first got here, people were still living in those matchbox houses or the later edition houses that weren't very good. Those houses have either been replaced or renovated with more insulation put in. Families are smaller now than they used to be so the homes are not as crowded. Most of the changes have been pretty good. Right now, if you look at the school we have and the recreational facilities—that's been a major change. There wasn't a lot to do here when I first came. We had the community hall, but that's all. Now, there's the arena, the gym, the golf course, the baseball diamonds. . . . We've always been a community that has community pride in itself. We're proud of our facilities, of the looks and appearance of the community as a whole. Generally, most of the yards are clean and tidy compared to some of the other communities in the Arctic. Whether it's lack of pride in the community or just the people—or where we are. We're kind of independent and we try to keep it that way.

Holman's best-known event is probably the yearly Holman Kingalik Jamboree, which started around 1968 as an outgrowth of Sports Day. On the first Sports Day, Shorty Brown, an organizer from Yellowknife, brought watermelons and ice cream, and although the ice cream disappeared quickly, no one touched the watermelons because they had never seen one before. Since that time, the jamboree has grown into a major event, lasting three days and involving dancing, feasting, and traditional Inuit activities such as bannock making, tea boiling, seal skinning, duck plucking, harpoon throwing, and so forth. People from all over the territories participate (or just observe), many staying in tents or in the homes of Holman residents. Family and friends separated by long distances get reacquainted. The Kingalik Jamboree occurs in June, on Father's Day weekend, which coincides with the spring migration of eider ducks into Prince Albert Sound. A high point of the event is the crowning of the king (kingalik, or male eider) and queen (mittik, or female eider) of the jamboree—individuals chosen by committee based upon their level of participation (not necessarily skill) in the games (Kane Tologanak 1991, personal communication). Over the years, there has also been an increase in the number of tourists coming to Holman just to attend the jamboree.

195

Fifty Years of Change

In 1989, Holman celebrated the fiftieth anniversary of its founding. As the final chapters of this book have indicated, much has
changed since the construction of the trading post in 1939.
Although the most obvious changes have been material and
economic, the residents of Holman have been profoundly influenced socially, politically, and attitudinally by their increased
exposure to the southern world. Some changes have been good:
improved health care, increased educational and occupational
opportunities, increased economic security, which has elimi-
nated the vagaries of famine and starvation. Other changes,
however, have been negative: alcohol and drug abuse, suicide,
spousal assault, unemployment, and underemployment.

Some Contemporary Voices

Young Holman resident, August 19, 1992. Going to outpost camp
for half the year, those were the best times. For me, that was
when we really started hunting, at thirteen. Hunting was always
a major part of my life when I was growing up. It's kind of
different nowadays. We stopped going when the [seal] prices
dropped, maybe when I was nineteen. Before Halahaqvik [out-
post camp in Prince Albert Sound], we used to go anywhere out
of town to a lot of different campgrounds, differing by year. It
used to be during spring and summer, and early fall, and then
we'd come back. This was from the time I was born until I was
twelve. We spent four or five years [after that] at Halahaqvik,
and we'd stay out of town for six months. Towards the end, I'd
miss town, when I was growing up and getting into girls. It never
got to the point where I was townsick, I guess.

Young Holman resident, November 13, 1992. I haven't been trapping since 1979, and I really miss it. I used to run a trapline with
my dad down Prince Albert Sound. I was always impressed with
how my dad always knew where the traps were even though it
might be dark out. Sometimes I would get disoriented but my
Dad would not. This year I'm trapping because I really want to
do it. I'm going to skin my own foxes. I'm not going to give them
to my mom. I've decided that this is something I want to do
myself.

Holman resident in his thirties, August 1994. There's a lot of
materialism now, these days. Long ago when I was a kid, before

there was TV and all kinds of toys, there were just wooden toys like your Dad would make for you. Now there's all kinds of toys and TV. We used to play out all day when I was a kid. Never worry about TV. Never worry about anything. Now, it seems like the kids don't know how to play out anymore. And when they do, they fight over all these new toys. They say "Mommy this" and "Mommy that," "Daddy this and Daddy that." It's not like long ago. We used to go play out on the edge of town. It seemed like it was far out of town. Now it seems so close because there's so much all over the place. It's really totally different. Even the attitudes of the people have changed with all this material stuff around. Long ago, it seemed like everybody cared for everybody else. Like it didn't matter to them what they shared or gave away. Now they have to watch what they share and give away because of all the money and everything costing so much. It's like they're forgetting how to share. Maybe it's because of all this material stuff. Long ago, there used to be hardly any booze. No drugs. Today, it seems like everywhere you go, you hear about it. There's too much drugs and booze in this town. It's sad to see it go that way. It used to be so peaceful.

Not enough people visit today like long ago. It seems the only people who go visiting are the elders. They still go visiting each other. You don't see middle-aged people visiting unless you invite them for supper or dinner or something. They don't come over on their own anymore. You have to ask them these days. It's not the same. Long ago, you'd just go visiting. It's just different from when I was growing up.

Holman resident in this thirties, September 20, 1992. I remember when I was younger, I used to travel with my dad by dogsled. We used to spend a good deal of time in the spring by Kaoraokut. My dad used to have to cross cracks in the sea ice which he did by getting pieces of ice to use as a bridge. I really remember those days. Traveling by dogs was so peaceful. I also think that the climate was warmer because I never got cold.

Young Holman resident, March 3, 1993. Do you notice that it seems like people don't visit anymore? Since everybody has a TV, people don't visit as much anymore. It used to be that people would come over and visit and stay for a long time and talk and have tea. And almost everybody would have food, too. Now, it's like people can come over for a little while, they watch TV, maybe have tea, and then they leave. Since everybody's watching TV, they hardly talk about anything either.

197

Holman hockey player, March 22, 1993. I started playing the year my mom came back from Inuvik with two hockey sticks. I must have been about twelve. We played in the street back then. I started skating when I was about thirteen, and I just learned by watching everybody else skate. My first pair of skates was size eleven, and I had two wool duffel liners in them so my feet would fit and stay warm. Joseph was worse—he had size thirteens. I just learned to play hockey by watching everybody else. We didn't even have televisions back then, and I never learned from TV. I probably learned everything I needed to know about hockey by the time we had it on TV.

Holman hockey player, March 22, 1993. We used to play lots in the spring, from about now [March] until May maybe. We used to play on King's Bay, but mostly on Father's Lake. It was mostly drop-in, and we used Ski-Doos for nets, but then we got smarter and made nets out of two-by-fours and plastic tarps as the mesh. David was the first one to get goalie pads. He made his own out of styrofoam and canvas, and they were just like real goalie pads, with panels and everything. I remember he showed up with them one time and everybody complained that he had some and the other goalie didn't, so he took one off and gave it to the other goalie, and they each played with one.

A community that becomes so rapidly integrated, politically, economically, and socially, with southern Canadian society cannot avoid the stresses characteristic of the wider society. Because of its small size and relative isolation compared with other northern communities, Holman has not been devastated by these maladaptive social and psychological trends as have places such as Coppermine, Cambridge Bay, Tuktoyaktuk, and Inuvik. Recognizing the urgency of dealing with growing social problems, Holman residents have organized educational pro-grams and "safe house" networks to confront alcohol abuse, drug abuse, AIDS infection, and domestic assault. It is also hoped that employment problems will be eased as other ave-nues for economic development are explored in the harvesting of renewable resources, the development of tourism, and the responsible exploitation of nonrenewable minerals and hydro-carbons. The outcome of these projects will largely define the Holman of the next fifty years.

Epilogue

A long time ago, there were people living in Prince Albert Sound. One year, the ice broke up early, and the people ended up on the islands. Those people of long ago—old timers—were out hunting seal. Some of them went out of their minds. They spent the summer there and ran out of food. They starved.

Frank Kuptana, 1991

THIS BOOK HAS only scratched the surface in relating the prehistory, history, and contemporary society of the Holman region. Many stories of the near and distant past will unfortunately never be told. On every island, peninsula, and river mouth, there are stories of joy, hardship, starvation, and conflict that can be traced to generations of Copper Inuit as well as to the Thule and Dorset peoples who came before them. Yet their memories have been blown away like snowflakes in a blizzard.

As one walks or snowmobiles over the tundra anywhere in the Holman region, it is impossible to fantasize being the first person ever to set foot in any given narrow valley, or the first to climb a cliff or mountain. At every strategic location, there is evidence of human occupation—a human presence that may have occurred ten years ago or two thousand years ago. A hunter or hiker who pauses beside a babbling stream in summer to

199

admire the scenery may be sitting at a location where many years ago people starved to death, or where a shaman performed a healing ceremony for an ailing child, or where two men fought to claim a woman as wife.

If these stories could be told, we would know more about the heart and soul of the Kangiryuarmiut people. Perhaps just knowing about the existence of countless generations that came before is enough to mark their memory, even if we don't know their names, where they were born, how they lived, and where they died. To their nameless memory and the memory of those now departed Holman elders that are known to us, this book is dedicated.

References Cited

Armstrong, Sir Alexander
    1857   *A Personal Narrative of the Discovery of the Northwest Passage.* Hurst and Blackett, London.

Berton, Pierre
    1988   *The Arctic Grail: The Quest for the North West Passage and the North Pole, 1818–1909.* Viking, New York.

Buliard, Roger
    1951   *Inuk.* Farrar Straus, New York.

Burnham, George
    1986   *The White Road.* Interlake Graphics, Winnipeg.

Collinson, Richard
    1889   *Journal of the Enterprise on the Expedition in Search of Sir John Franklin's Ships by Behring Strait, 1850–1855.* T. B. Collinson, ed. Sampson, Low, Marston, and Rivington, London.

Condon, Richard
    1983   *Inuit Behavior and Seasonal Change in the Canadian Arctic.* UMI Press: Ann Arbor.
    1987   *Inuit Youth: Growth and Change in the Canadian Arctic.* Rutgers University Press, New Brunswick, NJ.

Damas, David
    1975   "Demographic Aspects of Central Eskimo Marriage Practices. *American Ethnologist* 2(3):409–418.
    1984   "Copper Eskimo," in David Damas (ed.), *Handbook of North American Indians: Arctic.* Smithsonian Institution, Washington, D.C.

de Coccala, Raymond, and Paul King
    1986   *The Incredible Eskimo: Life Among the Barren Land Eskimo.* Hancock House, Surrey BC.

Dekin, A. A. Jr.
    1975   "Models of Pre-Dorset Culture: Towards an Explicit Methodology,"

Ph.D. dissertation, Department of Anthropology, Michigan State University.

Dumond, D. E.
1987   *The Eskimos and Aleuts.* Thames and Hudson, New York (revised paperback edition).

Farquharson, Don
1976   "Inuit Land Use in the West-Central Canadian Arctic," in Milton Freeman (ed.), *Report of the Inuit Land Use and Occupancy Project*, vol. 1. Department of Indian and Northern Affairs, Ottawa.

Finnie, Richard
1940   *The Lure of the North.* David McKay, Philadelphia.

Fort Brabant Journal
1927/1928   Hudson's Bay Company Archives, Winnipeg.

Fort Collinson Journal
1932   Hudson's Bay Company Archives, Winnipeg, Manitoba.

Godsell, Philip
1934   *Arctic Trader.* Travel Book Club, London.

Hickey, Cliff
1984   "An Examination of Processes of Social Change among Nineteenth Century Copper Inuit," *Etudes/Inuit/Studies* 8(1):13–36.

Hudson's Bay Company
1928   Annual Report, Western Arctic District. Hudson's Bay Company Archives, Winnipeg.

Jacobs, M. M. and J. B. Richardson
1983   *Arctic Life: Challenge to Survive.* Carnegie Museum of Natural History, Pittsburgh.

Jenness, Diamond
1922   *The Life of the Copper Eskimos.* Report of the Canadian Arctic Expedition, 1913–1918, vol. 12(a). Ottawa.
1928   *The People of the Twilight.* University of Chicago Press, Chicago.
1964   *Eskimo Administration: Canada.* Arctic Institute of North America Technical Paper No. 14. Arctic Institute of North America, Washington, D.C.
1991   *Arctic Odyssey: The Diary of Diamond Jenness, 1913–1916.* Stuart Jenness, ed. Canadian Museum of Civilization, Hull, Quebec.

Klengenberg, Christian
1932   *Klengenberg of the Arctic.* J. Cape, London.

Lowe, Ronald
1983   *Kangiryuarmiut Uqauhingita Numiktittitdjutingit.* Committee for Original People's Entitlement, Inuvik.

Maxwell, M. S.
1960   "An Archaeological Analysis of Eastern Grant Land, Ellesmere Island, N.W.T." In "Contributions to Anthropology in 1960," *National Museum of Canada Bulletin* 180:20–55, Ottawa.
1984   "Pre-Dorset and Dorset Prehistory of Canada," In *Handbook of North American Indians: Arctic.* D. Damas, ed. Smithsonian Institution Press, Washington DC (pp. 359–368).
1985   *Prehistory of the Eastern Arctic.* Academic Press, Orlando.

McClure, Robert
n.d.   *The Arctic Dispatches, Containing an Account of the Discovery of the North-west Passage.* J. D. Potter, London.

McGhee, Robert
  1972 *Copper Inuit Prehistory.* National Museum of Canada Publications in Archaeology, No. 2. Ottawa.
  1978 *Canadian Arctic Prehistory.* Van Nostrand Reinhold, Toronto.
  1983 "Eskimo Prehistory," In *Arctic Life: Challenge to Survive,* M. M. Jacobs and J. B. Richardson, eds. Carnegie Museum of Natural History, Pittsburgh (pp. 73–93).

Meldgaard, J.
  1962 "On the Formative Period of the Dorset Culture," In *Prehistoric Relations between the Arctic and Temperate Zones of North America.* J. M. Campbell, ed. Arctic Institute of North America Technical Paper 11, Montreal.

Metayer, Maurice, ed. and translator
  1966 *I, Nuligak.* Simon and Schuster, Markham, Ontario.

Morrison, David
  1991 "The Copper Inuit Soapstone Trade," *Arctic* 44(3):239–246.

Moyles, R. G.
  1979 *British Law and Arctic Men: The Celebrated 1917 Murder Trials of Sinnisiak and Uluksuk, First Inuit Tried Under White Man's Law.* Western Producer Prairie Books, Saskatoon.

Neatby, L.
  1960 "McClure and the Passage," *The Beaver,* winter: 33–41.

Park, Linda K.
  1990 "Mediating Cultures: An Ethnography of Art Production in Holman." M.A. thesis, University of Western Ontario, London, Ontario.

Rasmussen, Knud
  1932 "Intellectual Culture of the Copper Eskimos," *Report of the Fifth Thule Expedition 1921–1924.* Vol. 9. Gyldendalske Boghandel, Copenhagen.

Royal Canadian Mounted Police
  1931–1952 RCMP Patrol Reports, Coppermine Detachment. Public Archives of Canada, Ottawa.
  1952 Royal Canadian Mounted Police Annual Report, Coppermine Detachment. Public Archives of Canada, Ottawa.

Schwatka, Frederick
  1884 The Netschilluk Innuits. *Science* 4(98):543–545.

Sparling, Mary, and Don Snowdon
  1978 Interview with Father Tardy, Holman Island, December 6. Unpublished manuscript on file at the Inuit Art Section of the Department of Indian and Northern Affairs, Hull, Quebec.

Stefansson, Vilhjalmur
  1906 Anglo-American Expedition Diary, 1906–1907. Dartmouth College Library, Special Collections, Hanover, NH.
  1913 *My Life with the Eskimo.* Macmillan, New York.
  1919 The Stefansson-Anderson Arctic Expedition of the American Museum: Preliminary Ethnological Report. *Anthropological Papers of the American Museum of Natural History* 14(1). New York.
  1921 *The Friendly Arctic: The Story of Five Years in Polar Regions.* Macmillan, N.Y.
  1928 "The 'Blond' Eskimos," *Harpers Magazine* 156:191–198.

References Cited

Tardy, Henri
  1979 "The Beginnings of the Holman Island Co-op," *Inuktitut Magazine,*
        Winter:68–75.
Taylor, W. E. Jr.
  1967 "Summary of Archaeological Field Work on Banks and Victoria Is-
        lands, Arctic Canada, 1965," *Arctic Anthropology* 4:221–243.
Taylor, W. E. Jr., and G. Swinton
  1967 "Prehistoric Dorset Art," *The Beaver* 298:32–47.
Usher, Peter
  1965 *Economic Basis and Resource Use of the Coppermine-Holman Region.*
        (NRC65-2). Ottawa, Department of Northern Affairs and National
        Resources, Northern Coordination and Research Centre.
  1971 *The Bankslanders: Economy and Ecology of a Frontier Trapping Com-
        munity.* 3 volumes. (NSRG71-1). Ottawa, Department of Northern
        Affairs and National Resources, Northern Coordination and Re-
        search Centre.
Webster, J. Harold
  1980 *Arctic Adventure.* Dominion Press, Ontario.
Wenzel, George
  1991 *Animal Rights, Human Rights: Ecology, Economy, and Ideology in
        the Canadian Arctic.* University of Toronto Press, Toronto.

Index

*Illustrations are indicated by **boldface** type.*

205